INDIA THREE THOUSAND YEARS AGO

OR

THE SOCIAL STATE OF THE A'RYAS ON THE BANKS OF THE INDUS IN THE TIMES OF THE VEDAS

BEING THE EXPANSION OF A LECTURE DELIVERED IN THE TOWNHAL OF BOMBAY BEFORE THE MECHANICS' INSTITUTION, 1858.

INDIA THREE THOUSAND YEARS AGO

OR

THE SOCIAL STATE OF THE A'RYAS ON THE BANKS OF THE INDUS IN THE TIMES OF THE VEDAS

BEING THE EXPANSION OF A LECTURE DELIVERED IN THE TOWNHAL OF BOMBAY BEFORE THE MECHANICS' INSTITUTION, 1858.

BY

JOHN WILSON, D.D., F.R.S.

HONORARY PRESIDENT OF THE BOMBAY BRANCH OF THE ROYAL ASIATIC SOCIETY, AND MISSIONARY OF THE FREE CHURCH OF SCOTLAND.

GYAN

Published by

GYAN

Gyan Publishing House
5, Ansari Road
Daryaganj, New Delhi-110002
Phone: 011-47034999, 9811692060
E-mail: books@gyanbooks.com

Distribution Network
gyanbooks.com
India, USA, Canada, UK, Australia, France

ISBN : 978-81-212-2802-2 (HB)
First Published, 1858

2nd Impression 2021

Printed at: Gyan Press, Delhi.

India Three Thousand Years Ago
Author: John Wilson

INDIA THREE THOUSAND YEARS AGO

OR

THE SOCIAL STATE OF THE A'RYAS ON THE BANKS OF THE INDUS IN THE TIMES OF THE VEDAS:

BEING THE EXPANSION OF A LECTURE DELIVERED IN THE TOWNHAL OF BOMBAY BEFORE THE MECHANICS' INSTITUTION, 1858.

BY JOHN WILSON, D.D., F.R.S.,

HONORARY PRESIDENT OF THE BOMBAY BRANCH OF THE ROYAL ASIATIC SOCIETY, AND MISSIONARY OF THE FREE CHURCH OF SCOTLAND.

BOMBAY:

SMITH, TAYLOR AND CO.

LONDON : SMITH, ELDER AND CO., 55 CORNHILL.

EDINBURGH : W. WHYTE AND CO.

M.DCCC.LVIII.

TO THE RIGHT HONORABLE

JOHN, LORD ELPHINSTONE, G.C.H.,

GOVERNOR OF BOMBAY,

etc. etc. etc.

MY LORD,

It was under the auspices of your Lordship's considerate and vigorous government that the Course of public Lectures,—designed for the purpose of literary and scientific instruction,—of the first of which the following pages form an expansion, was delivered in the Townhall of Bombay, at the commencement of the present year, in connexion with our local Mechanics' Institution. On this account, I am well disposed to offer this little brochure for your Lordship's acceptance. I have other reasons, however, for presenting you with this simple, though inadequate, token of my respect and regard. Like your distinguished relative, the Honorable Mountstuart Elphinstone,—whose name is associated in the West of India with all that is judicious and disinterested in British administration, as applied to a state of oriental society, fashioned, moulded, and guided by principles, which, though requiring improvement or change, demand the most attentive observation and study of all who have to deal with them,—you have long taken a particular interest in all geographical description, and antiquarian and historical research, calculated to throw light on the past and present condition of this great country, and of the numerous tribes and tongues which form its diversified population. Few, if any, of our statesmen have seen and learned so much of India as yourself, not only in connexion with your public deliberation and movements as the head of the Madras and Bombay Presidencies respectively, but as an intelligent and enterprizing traveller among the valleys and mountains to the north of India, in which its earliest inhabitants were first established, and which, from age to age, have first witnessed the advent of the fresh Asiatic tribes which have sought to participate in its reputed riches or to acquire its coveted sovereignty. To our learned Societies and Educational Institutions in Bombay, you have personally given every assistance which could be reasonably expected or even desired. The public Economic and General Museum, now forming in the midst of us, has enjoyed your constant and effective direction and patronage. "The Bombay Selections," published since the commencement of your Lordship's present administration, contain a mass of statistical, ethnographical, and geographical information of the most valuable character. To your Lordship's enlightened zeal and constant advocacy, the great public works advancing throughout our various provinces, which are most palpable symbols to the natives of the resources of the British government and people, are deeply indebted. Your Lordship's judgment, forethought, vigilance, promptitude, decision, and courage, with that effective coöperation of public agency which they have selected and harmonized, have, by the blessing of God, whose gifts they are, instrumentally contributed much, as everywhere acknowledged, to preserve the threatened peace of the West of India during the season of this awful affliction which has been sent to other districts of this great country.

In the little work which, in association with your Lordship's name, and at the request of the Institution before which it was delivered, I now lay before the public, I have endeavoured to glean from the oldest compositions of the Hindus, the Vedas, and especially from the first of them, the Ṛig-Veda,—of which two of the others, the Sáma and Yajur are principally extracts, while the fourth, the Atharvan, is of much later origin,—the general information which they contain concerning the earliest state of Indian society, particularly as it bears on the illustration of that of later times. In doing this I have availed myself of the various translations mentioned in the notes which I have subjoined, but constantly referred, also, in all matters of importance, to the works of our greatest orientalists who have made the most important discoveries in Indian antiquities, and to the original Sanskrit text of the Vedas and their *Bháshyas*, or Commentaries, from my own study and investigation of which, made in their more important connexions with the opinions, institutions, and practices of the Hindus, I have drawn, as will be seen, to a considerable extent. My desire has been to give, as far as practicable within the restricted range assigned to me, a personal contribution to the First Chapter of Indian History. Those who best know the limited historical material at the disposal of the Indian student, and the bulky and obscure volumes from which it has to be drawn, will give the most credit for any success which may have been experienced in this attempt. The ancient Vedas, which consist of Odes and Hymns addressed to the divinities which they recognized, contain but few allusions which can be made to bear on the illustration of the external history of the A'ryas, who so long proved the ruling tribe in India, and whose assumed superiority among the various peoples domiciled in this great country is still to be observed to the present day. But those remarkable compositions, here and there, throw most interesting light on the social and religious state of that people shortly after their settlement on the banks of the Indus and its affluents. To the times of the Vedic compositions the following judgment of Mr. Gladstone is, mutatis mutandis, precisely applicable:—"In much that this Homeric world exhibits, we see the taint of sin at work, but far, as yet, from its perfect work and its ripeness; it stands between paradise and the vices of later heathenism, far from both, from the latter as well as from the former." The educated natives of India, I am thoroughly convinced, from all that I know of their views and feelings, will admit this fact; and they will readily abandon the position which their countrymen occupy with reference to the influence and authority of later Hinduism. With this movement, however, they will not be contented; for even on the Vedas a permanent resting-place cannot possibly be found. The patronage given by government to the publication, and translation, and exposition of the Vedas and their kindred literature, will thus have a moral effect throughout the whole of India, incalculably exceeding in value the money which has been spent in this enterprize. This patronage has hitherto reflected great credit on the East India Company, through whose administration this wondrous eastern empire has been founded; and it will doubtless be continued by the imperial administration which has just commenced, and for a blessing on which, to the enlightenment and elevation of India, many prayers, offered up in the prevailing name of the Purchaser and Prince of Peace, are rising for a memorial before God.

For the opinions expressed throughout this pamphlet, I am, of course, alone responsible. Since the last sheet of it got into type, I have received the third volume of Professor H. H. Wilson's Translation of the Ṛig-Veda; and I have been gratified to find that it fully warrants the deductions which I have made from those portions of the Veda,—the third and fourth Ashṭaks, or Ogdoads,—which that volume embraces. Throughout the Lecture I have given my authorities, adding some illustrative notes which may not be without their value to certain classes of readers.

Begging your Lordship to excuse this intrusion, I am, my Lord,

Yours with great respect and regard,

JOHN WILSON.

BOMBAY, OCTOBER, 1858.

CONTENTS.

PRINCIPAL NOTES.

INDIA THREE THOUSAND YEARS AGO.

THE India of the present day and the India of ancient times differ very much in their extent and productions, and connexions with the other nations of the world. The India of the present day includes the whole country lying between the Hindu Kush and the Himâlaya mountains on the north and the island of Ceylon on the south; and between the coasts of Sindh, Gujarât, the Konkan, and Malabar on the west, and the confines of China, Burmah, and the shores of Orissa and Coromandel on the east. The area of that portion of it which belongs to the British Government and its Allies is mentioned, in a late Parliamentary Return, as amounting to 1,465,322 (or, in round numbers, a million and a half) square miles.* Among its ranges and clusters of picturesque hills and sublime and gigantic mountains, the highest in the world, and over its vast and oceanic plains, there is a population, of multitudinous races and tribes, estimated at from a hundred and eighty to two hundred millions of souls, and actually not probably falling short of

* Statistical Tables relating to the Colonial and other Possessions of the United Kingdom, (1857) p. 8. The number of square miles, here mentioned, is exclusive of certain of the Portuguese and French territories entered as "not known."

the larger of these numbers.* It possesses every variety of climate, ranging from almost unendurable cold to unendurable heat. The fertilizing rains of heaven,—evaporated from its surrounding oceans, condensed on its lofty eminences, and precipitated by its tropical atmospheric agitation,—descend upon a large portion of it with a copiousness which there is scarcely room enough to receive, while a powerful sun renders them in their season a surprizing source of vivification and productiveness;† though portions of it, especially on the borders of Rájputáná, are rainless districts, and form only a fearful desert, like the valley of the shadow of death, the *Marusthal*‡ of its own people. Viewed in totality, it is a country of remarkable natural richness and capability. Its principal river systems, rising on its northern heights and platforms, and flowing both to the south-west, as that of the Indus and its affluents, and to the south-east, as those of the Ganges and Brahmapu-

* In the Blue Book above referred to, p. 8, the population of India is stated at 180,367,148, being thirty millions in excess of that set forth by the East India Company only three or four years ago. There is reason to believe that even this estimate of a hundred and eighty millions is fully twenty millions short of the reality. E. g., the Native States under Bombay, exclusive of Kachh, Káṭhiáwaḍ, and Kolápur, are given at only 2,000,934, which certainly cannot include all the population of the Baroda territories properly so called, of the districts of Pattan and Khaḍi, and of the tributaries in the Revákántá, Mahikántá, Pálanpur, Southern Maráthá Country, and other Agencies. Similar shortcomings in reckoning are elsewhere apparent.

† For notices of the Principal Falls of Rain in India, see an excellent paper by Dr. Buist on the Physical Geography of India, in the Transactions of the Bombay Geographical Society, 1856-1857.

‡ The Region-of-death, applied to a desert.

tra, are unequalled in the olden continents, and of great importance both for irrigation and navigation; while its secondary river systems, as those rising from the Vindhyádri and Sahyádri, and flowing to the west and southeast, promise to reward the enterprize and industry of man, now devoting them in part to these important objects under servants of the British Government distinguished alike by science and philanthropy.* Its vegetable productions, ministering both to the necessities and luxuries of its people, sustain the majority of its inhabitants, even without the use of animal food. Their clothing is derived from one of its humble perennial plants. Their houses are in many instances constructed from the branches and leaves of a single tree, which may have grown at their own doors. The material of the instruments of their labour is ready for their hands throughout the length and breadth of the land. They tread, in some districts, on mineral treasures of the useful metals and of coal, the vital aliment of machinery, on both its cultivated and uncultivated fields. Its "kings barbaric" have their "pearl and gold;" and its jewels and gems shine and sparkle in the palaces of the great in the lands of civilization and refinement. It exchanges its commodities with foreign lands, recognizing the commercial fellowship of the nations of the earth; but it does this more for convenience than from economic constraint. If supplies are brought to it from afar, it is more because its people lay not hold of them at hand than because of any natural destitution of them within its own borders. The annual public re-

* Colonel Arthur Cotton, of the Madras Engineers, and Lieutenant Haig, and other assistants trained by him in connexion with the great waterworks of Rajámandarí, Tanjur, etc.

venue of the portion of it belonging to Britain, is about thirty millions sterling; while its public debt, which could probably be cleared at once by available assets, is less than the product of two years of this revenue.* Its exports are of the most valuable and abundant character; and they are conveyed from it, to considerably upwards of a million and a half tons annually, even to the most distant parts of the earth. A large and continuous current of wealth is flowing into it from the west.† It is now sharing the benevolent solicitude, as it is enjoying the government,—which it has not yet learned adequately to appreciate,—of the most enlightened and philanthropic nation of the world.

The India of ancient times, of which we are to treat this evening, had no such magnitude and importance. It was only the country of the river Indus, from which it received its name—afterwards applied to the whole land, the boundaries of which we have just mentioned. It was only, or principally, the *Panchanada,* the Pentapotamia of the Greeks, or Panjáb, the Land-of-the-five-waters of later times, comprising the districts of the affluents of the Indus, denominated in the ancient Sanskrit the *Sindhuḥ,* or *Sindhus,* of which *Indus* is the equivalent, the sibilant letter *s* having been transmuted, according to well-known usage, into *h,* easily

* The revenue of the Indian Government amounted in 1855 to £ 29,133,000, while its debt at the same date was only £55,531,120.

† The tonnage of the imports into India (exclusive of that of native craft) for the year ending April 1855 was 1,637,379 tons; while that of the Exports was 1,614,877 tons. The value of the Imports for this year was £14,470,92, and that of the Exports was £20,194,255, the balance in trade in favour of India being thus £5,773,328, nearly six millions sterling.

elided by a people like the Greeks, too little careful like ourselves of orthoëpical precision. The land of the INDUS was the original INDIA; and to speak of our leaving India to go to Sindh, or the Panjáb, is as consummate nonsense as for a Northumbrian to say that he leaves England when he goes to the districts of ancient Anglia. Ancient India did not comprehend a twentieth part of the territory or resources of what is now Modern India. Its people were ignorant of the great and opulent continent, to which the conquests of their descendants in after times were destined to extend, in which the intelligence and activity of their race were to be developed, and in which trial was to be made of their ability to elevate or depress the tribes who had gone before them, and who were the first of the human family to behold the natural wonders and to taste the providential bounties by which we are still surrounded.

So much for prefatorial and geographical explanation. A word now in chronological and ethnographical exposition. We have entitled our lecture, "India Three Thousand Years Ago: or the Social State of the A'ryás on the Banks of the Indus in the Time of the Vedas." We have done this with deliberation and becoming literary warrant. Amidst the mass of wild and reckless legendary matter contained in the ancient writings of the Indians and Singhalese, one or two points of time have been ascertained with precision. One of the most important of these is the death, in the year 544 or 543 before Christ, of Shákya Muni, the founder of Buddhism, a system of daring and erroneous speculation which ascribes all existences and changes to simple nature and growth, viewed without reference to an all-wise and all-powerful Creator, or to a directing and sustaining Providence; and which represents the highest good of man as realizable in the extinction of his distinctive spiritual being.* A tendency to this system of thought, but not fully developed or organized, is seen in other writings, as those of Kapila Muni, the founder of the Sánkhya, or Numeral, System of Indian Philosophy, which in its origin must consequently be older than Buddhism. Both the primitive Sánkhya and the Buddhist writings, and also the more ancient authorities of two other Schools of Philosophy preceding them in point of time, recognize the existence of a body of poetical literature called the VEDAS. One of these schools of philosophy now alluded to, the Purva (or Prior) Mímánsá professes to seek an orthodox interpretation of the Vedas, thus recognizing them as ancient works of authority; and the latter, the Uttara (or Lower) Mímánsá, or Vedáṇta, professes to accomplish their "end" or "object" simply by a pantheistic recognition of the Divine Spirit alleged to be the only Entity, thus showing considerable progress in speculation since the time of the origination of the Vedas.† These schools of philosophy also refer to Liturgical prose works, the Bráhmaṇas, associated with the Vedas and professedly comprehended under their name, but found, both by their diction and style and ways of applying the poeti-

* On the date of the death of Shákya Muni, or Buddha (the comprehending-Intelligence), see the satisfactory Comparison of the Northern and Southern Buddhist Chronologies in Lassen's Indische Alterthumskunde, the great standard work on Indian Antiquities.

† For a brief view of the Six Schools of Indian Philosophy, see Lecture by the author, delivered at the request of the Bombay Dialectic Society.

cal Vedas to be posterior to them by at least two or three centuries. The Vedas, it is observed, are themselves collections of different poetical pieces of varying age; and an interval of some extent must have occurred between their composition and formation into Collections, or *Sanhitás*, arranged on different principles of construction.* In this way we are carried back by a legitimate

* The word Veda may be rendered Fount-of-Knowledge or of Vision, the Sanskrit root of the name *vid* or *vidh*, appearing in the Greek εἰδεω and εἰδω, Latin *vido* and *video*, and English *wit*.

The *Ṛig-Veda*, the oldest of the four Vedas has its some 11,000 distichs, or *ṛich*, from which it receives its name, arranged in hymns according to their authors and the gods whom they invoke. The *Yajur Veda*, the Sanhitá of which is called the Vájasaneya, and which has about half the number of distichs found in the Ṛik or Ṛig, derives about half its material from the Ṛig. The *Sáma Veda*, which is only about half the size of the Yajur, draws almost its whole contents from the Ṛig, selecting them in small portions from particular hymns and arranging them principally for sacrificial chaunting. The distichs, or verses, of the *Atharva-Veda*,—which is posterior to the others in composition,—including a few of the later hymns of the Ṛig, and dealing principally in incantations and curses, are nearly, according to Dr. Roth, its learned Editor, as numerous as those of the Ṛig. For interesting information on the arrangements of the Vedas, see Dr. R. Roth, Zur Litteratur und Geschiste des Wed; and for an Index to the passages occurring in the Vedas respectively, see a paper by W. D. Whitney in the Indische Studien of Dr. A. Weber, vol. ii. 321-368.

Dr. Roth founds an ingenious argument for the antiquity of the Vedas on the ancient grammatical and others helps to their interpretation and recitation. The Prátishákhya Sútras, containing simple rules of Sanskrit, and particularly, Vedic Grammar, he assigns to the fifth or end of the sixth century before Christ. These Sútras mention the Schools of Sákala and others as the compilers of the Vedic collection in such a way as to show that that collection cannot fall later than the seventh century before Christ. The composition of the Hymns of the Vedas must have preceded their collection by several

criticism, to a period stretching probably between the fifteenth and twelfth centuries before Christ, a period, even on its side proximate to ourselves, fully "three thousand years ago." That period, it must be evident, is the most interesting in Indian history; for it is in it that we find the germ of the Indian nation and Indian institutions. As connected with India it was till late nearly wholly unknown to the dwellers in the orient as well as in the occident. The Indians though they sung or chaunted the Vedas, as they still do in their privileged worship, did not look to them with intelligence for information respecting their fathers and country; for, in conformity with their bewildering traditional veneration of them and the dicta of their later writings, they held that they had come in their complete form from the four mouths of their god Brahmá.* They withheld them as long as possible

centuries. Again, Yáska an old grammarian, the author of the Nighaṇṭu and Nirukta, expository works on the Vedas, and who flourished a considerable time before Páṇini (placed by Dr. Roth 350 B. C.) refers to the Bráhmaṇas, or finished liturgical works on the Vedas, in such a way as to recognize them as works of antiquity in his own day. To the age of the Bráhmaṇas, we must add the time which must have intervened between their formation and the formation of the Vedic Collections, which are themselves not all of the same age, that of the Atharva Veda, in particular, being more modern than the rest. Making suitable allowances of time for the formation of the Bráhmaṇas, and for the several Collections of the Vedas, we are carried back for the origin of their hymns to a time such as that we have indicated above. This argument, considering its source, is entitled to great respect. Yet, the age of the grammatical auxiliaries to the interpretation of the Vedas requires a more extensive elimination than has yet been made.

* See, e. g., Bhágavata Purána, Skanda iii. 12. 30,37-39. Manu (i. 23.) says the three primordial Vedas were milked by the Supreme Ruler from Fire, the Air, and the Sun (अग्नि, वायु, रवि.)

from the curiosity and intelligence of the west. European gold and European importunity, however, have, principally in our own day, secured their possession;* and European learning and European ingenuity, with partial assistance from the natives of India and the writings they have received from their fathers, are securing their interpretation. They are all now in the process of being published and translated, by learned Britons, Frenchmen, Germans, and Americans, the East India Company being the chief patron of the work of their manifestation to the world.†

On opening the Vedas we find that the people of whom they treat, or rather whose religious services they embody, are called *A'ryá.* This word, the Bráhmanical commentators on the Vedas, and subsequent literary works, render by "respectable men." The text of the Vedas proves, however, that it is not, as there principally employed, a simple qualifying denominative, but a patronymic name, simply indicative of an *Aryan people.*‡

* The MS. copy of the Ṛig-Veda now in my possition for many years, and which I originally acquired for J. S. Law, Esq., of the Bombay Civil Service, is a Christian trophy, surrendered by a Bráhman convert to Christianity, baptized at Bankot by the Rev. James Mitchell.

† Three volumes of a critical edition of the Ṛig-Veda in Sanskrit, with the commentary of Sáyaṇa A'chárya, have been published, under the auspices of the East India Company, by the learned Dr. Max Müller of Oxford, who has devoted ten busy years to the work of editing them. His task is scarcely yet half finished. The translation of the Ṛig-Veda, by professor H. H. Wilson, proceeds as the original text appears.

‡ I have noticed instances, even in the Ṛig-Veda, in which the word *árya* seems to be used in the sense of "high, or respectable;"

The orientalist at once recognizes it as the equivalent of the *Airya* of the Pársís, as in the first fargard of the Vendidád and other places, in which *Airya vaéjo,* or the "pure Airya,"—the *Ariana* of the Greeks and eastern *Irán* of later times,—is spoken of; as in the Yashts, and other liturgical pieces, in which it is coupled with *Túirya* or *Turán,* a neighbouring country; and as in the Behistun tablets, deciphered and translated by Sir Henry Rawlinson, Professor Westergaard and Mr. Norris.* It was probably the ultimate extension of the name A'rya to the land of the Veda which led to the distinction made by the Zoroastrians of the "pure" or "original" Airya,—now referred to,—from which the original tribes of Irán had their dispersion.

That the A'ryás, in the time of the Vedas, were not in their primitive country is, I think, evident from several considerations. They counted their years by "winters," indicating a country in which the cold season was peculiarly marked.† They laid great stress on the *ashvamedha,* or horse-sacrifice, like the northern tribes. Compared with their neighbours

but this is perhaps a figurative use of the word, according to the well-known analogy of our adjective "frank," expressive of the qualities strikingly exhibited in the Frank people. In the event of *arya,* or *árya,* in the sense of "high" or "respectable" being the origin of the name of the country, *A'rya* is probably equivalent to "Highlands."

* In the ancient Persian tablets it reads *Ariya,* and in the Scythian tablets, *Arriya.*

† Dr. Stevenson, was, I believe, the first person to direct attention to this fact. See his Translation of the Sáma-Veda, p. 86. In addition to this translation of the Sáma, we have that of Dr. Benfey, in German, accompanied by a critical apparatus.

they had a white or fair complexion. They were not fully or peaceably established in the territories in which they were then found. The facts to which I have now referred have not escaped the notice of the learned and cautious translator of the Ṛig-Veda, Professor H. H. Wilson. "That they [the ancient Indians,] he says, had extended themselves from a more northern race is rendered probable from the peculiar expression used, on more than one occasion, in soliciting long life,—when the worshipper asks for a hundred *winters (himas)* a boon not likely to be desired by the natives of a warm climate. They appear also to have been a fair complexioned people, at least comparatively, and foreign invaders of India, as it is said that Indra [the god of the Ether or Firmament] divided the fields among his *white*-complexioned friends after destroying the indigenous Barbarian races, for such there can be little doubt we are to understand by the expression *Dasyu,* which so often recurs, and which is often defined to signify one who not only does not perform religious rites but attempts to harass their performers."* The Dasyus, here mentioned, are doubtless the *Daqyus* of the Pársí sacred writings, and the *Dahyas* of the Behistun tablets, rendered by "countries" or "provinces," probably of an exterior position like the Goim or Gentiles of the Hebrews. They were not altogether Barbarians; for they had distinctive cities and other establishments of at least a partial civilization, though the A'ryás, lately from more bracing climes than those which

* Wilson's Ṛig-Veda, vol. i. p. xlii.

they inhabited, proved too strong for them. The A'ryás of the Vedas, found, or made, other human enemies for themselves besides these Dasyus, or perhaps human enemies included under the general denomination of Dasyu, but with other more special names, Among these are to be particularly mentioned a people, often alluded to, called *Rákshasas,* from whom they suffered much, and who by their descendants were transferred in idea to the most distant south, and treated by them as a race of mythical giants; the *Ugras,* afterwards the typical representatives of fierce or cruel giants;* the *Pishá-chas,* viewed in later times as a set of mischievous and frolicsome devils; and the *Asuras,* afterwards looked to as wicked spirits, though they are thus spoken of in the Veda, "Encountering the (Asuras) carrying off Dabhíti he [Indra] burnt all their weapons in a kindled fire, and enriched the prince with their cattle, their horses, and their chariots."† Among peoples hostile to the A'ryás, we also find noticed the *Ajásas, Yakshas, Shigravas,*‡ *Kikaṭas,*§ and others. The enemies of the

* According to the system of the mixed castes set forth in Manu (x. 9), the *Ugra* is fictionally sprung from a Kshatriya male and a Shúdra woman.

† Wilson's Ṛig-Veda, vol. ii. pp. 245–246; Müller, vol. ii. 487. Asura, as afterwards noticed, means Lord. The giving of this name to a tribe is analogous to what we see in the case of Náyaka, of a similar meaning (Dux,) applied to the aboriginal tribe of the Náyaka-ḍás, east of Baroda.

‡ Ṛig-Veda, 5th Asht. 2 adh. warga, 27.

§ The Kíkaṭas are denonimated *nichas* or vile people, a form of expression much used since the Caste system has been established. Ṛig-Veda, Asht. iii. adh. 3. w. 21.

A'ryás are sometimes expressly mentioned as having a black skin: "He [Indra] punished for man those wanting religious rites; he tore off their black skin.* The Pisháchas are said to have been tawny-coloured.†

At the time at which the earlier portions of the Vedas were composed, the A'ryás, as we have already hinted, obviously inhabited the banks of the various affluents of the Indus and the province now denominated the Panjáb. Though Sáyaṇa A'chárya, the great Bráhmanical commentator on the Vedas, who flourished so late as the fourteenth century after Christ, interprets the rivers mentioned in the Vedas as the great streams of modern India, the text of the Veda gives him no authority for so doing. The rivers of the Vedas seem all to have been before the immediate observation of the writers of the Hymns (*Súktas*) of which the Collection of the Ṛig-Veda is composed. "Thou Indra hast rescued the kine, thou hast won the Soma juice; thou hast let loose the *seven rivers* to flow."‡ "Thou didst traverse *ninety and nine streams* like a hawk." His exploits are most glorious, in that he has replenished the *four rivers* of sweet water, spread over the surface of the earth."§ "All (sacrificial) viands concentrate in Agni [the god of fire] as the *seven great rivers* [united] flow into the ocean."‖ In the Panjáb, we have four, or five, or seven, or more, great rivers, ac-

* त्वचं कृष्णामरंधयत् Müller's Ṛig-Veda, vol. ii. p. 72.

† Ibid. p. 89. Wilson's Ṛig-Veda, vol. ii. p. 44. One worshipper in the Veda asks for himself a tawny-hued son.

‡ Wilson's Ṛig-Veda, vol. i. p. 88. See also, p. 99.

§ Ibid. p. 168. ‖ Ibid. p. 189.

cording as we cross it to the north or south. It is probably this district which is denominated in the Vendidád of the Pársís, the *Hapta Heñdu** or Seven Indies, the word Heñdu springing, as is obvious, from the *Sindhu*, the Sanskrit name of the Indus. Indeed, the Indus, is specifically mentioned in the Veda as that river on the banks of which some of the composers of the Vedas actually lived. Thus, we have, "May *Sindhu*, the renowned bestower of wealth hear us (fertilizing our) broad fields with water."† "I repeat with a (willing) mind the praises of Bhávya [a king] dwelling on the banks of the *Sindhu*."‡ In one of the hymns of the Ṛig-Veda, three specific streams are thus mentioned as connected with the worshippers of the Vedas:—"Gloriously shine forth, O Agni, in the places in which the descendants of Manu inhabit, on the banks of the *Dṛishadvatí*, the *A'payá*, and the *Sarasvatí*."§ These streams, I am of opinion, are connected with the south-western and not with the south-eastern system of Indian rivers. Two of them are thus noticed by Manu: "The country between the divine rivers Sarasvatí and Dṛishadvatí

* Vendidád, 1st fargard.

† Sáyaṇa Achárya, as hinted by Prof. Wilson, Ṛig-Veda, ii. p. 3, understands by the word Sindhu here, जलाभिमानी देवः, the god presiding over waters. Even in this sense, however, it is nothing but the personified Indus.

‡ सिंधावधि· Ṛig-Veda, 2nd asht, 1st adh. 11th w.

§ दृषद्वत्यां मानुष आपयायां सरस्वत्यां रेवदग्ने दिदीहि. Text of Ṛig-Veda by Müller, vol. ii. p. 747. I have not seen the translation of this part of the Veda by Prof. Wilson, who may probably have appended to it an illustrative note.

formed by the gods, is called *Brahmávarta*."* The Sarasvatí is the Sarsutí north-west of Tháneshar (Sthán-eshvar), as noticed by Professor Wilson in his Vishnu Purána.† It seems, from the manner in which it is sometimes spoken of in the Vedas, to have been a favorite with the A'ryás;‡ and this probably because of some resemblance,—such perhaps as that of losing itself in the sands, for it etymologically means a lake,—which it bore to the *Haraqaiti*, a river in the original Airya, of which it was the namesake.|| The Dṛishadvatí is supposed to have been in the neighbourhood of the Sarasvatí. I am not aware that the A'payá has been identified, though it may be the Vipápá, mentioned in the Mahábhárata§ along with the Dṛishadvatí and Vipáshá.

* Manu ii. 17. Sir William Jones says, "frequented by the gods;" but the original is देवनिर्मित, formed by the gods.

† Wilson's Vishnu Purána, p. 180.

‡ Vasiṣhṭha devotes to it alone two hymns in the 5th aṣhṭaka of the Ṛig-Veda.

|| For the identification of the name *Haraqaiti* with *Saraswati*, we are indebted to Burnouf (Commentaire sur le Yaçna, Notes et E'claircissements, p. xcii.) From *Haraqaiti*, the district of *Arachotia* of the Greeks (Arrian. Exped. Alex. iii. cap. 23; Strab. lib. xv. c. 2; Dionys. Perieg. v. 1096; Plin. lib. vi. cap. 25) derived its name. Burnouf, while ascribing a common origin to the names *Haraqaiti* and *Sarasvati*, felt unable to say whether Persia or India can claim the original. Noticing, however, the district of *Harôyo*, mentioned in the Vendidád of the Pársís, and identifying the word with *Sarayu*, the name of an Indian river (now the *Sarju*, afterwards mentioned in this lecture,) he justly observes that the Zend *Harôyo* is the more ancient form of the word as far as the vowels are concerned. (p. ciii, et seq.)

§ Bhishma Parva, ii. 342. Langlois, in his translation of the Ṛig-Veda, tom. ii. p. 230, says, "Je ne sais quelle est la riviére qui portait la nomme d' Apaya.

In another of the hymns of the Ṛig-Veda, the rivers *Vipáṭ*,—the equivalent according to etymology and to the Brahmanical commentator on the Veda, of the *Vipáshá* of the Mahábhárata, and the origin of the present *Beás*, —the *Hyphasis* or *Bibasis* of the Greeks,—and the *Chhutudrí*,—in later times the *Shatudrí* or *Satlej*,—are mentioned as holding a conversation with the sage Vishvámitra, the author of many of the Vedic hymns.* The *Vipáshí* and the dwellers on the *Vitastá*,—the *Hydaspes*, or Jhelum,—and the *Saryu*, (whether that near Ayodhyá or not is uncertain), are mentioned in a hymn of Vámdeva.† It is thus seen that the Panjáb and its neighbourhood formed the original habitat of the Indian A'ryás. The rivers of the south-eastern system are brought to notice in the more advanced portions of the Ṛig-Veda. The *Yamuná* and the *Gomatí* are first mentioned by Shayávásbva, "a descendant of Atri," in the fourth Aṣhṭaka.‡ The *Gangá* (Ganges) is only once mentioned and that in the eighth or last Aṣhṭaka.§

* Ṛig-Veda, Müller's text, vol. ii. p. 828.

† Ṛig-Veda 3d. adh. 6th. asht. 20th-22d. w.

‡ Ṛig-Veda 4th. ashtak, 3rd adhy. (Müller, ii. 452.) The *Yamuná* is also mentioned by Vasiṣhtha, viewed by the Hindu legends as a contemporary of Vishvámitra, Ṛig-Veda, 15th asht. 2d. adh. S. 15, 19th. dis. 17. 19.

§ This is in a hymn addressed to the personified Rivers, the 4th of the 3rd adhy. In this hymn the *Sindhu* (which is in the masculine gender, while all the others are in the feminine) is spoken of as the chief river. With it are invoked other rivers in the following order :—*Gangá*; *Yamuná*; *Sarasvatí*; *Shutudrí*, with the *Paruṣhní*, the Hydraotes from "Irávatí;" the *Asikní* the Chandrabhága, (identified from the "Akesines," as by Lassen) and the *Marudvṛidhá*; the *Vitastá* (Hydaspes for Vidaspes); the *Arjíkíya*,

I have seen no allusion to the tiger in the Vedas, though occasional mention is made in them of the lion. This is a presumption that the Ṛiṣhis, at the time of their composition, had not yet reached the land of the tiger. The distinctive lake Sharyáṇávatí is sometimes mentioned as in the dominions of the pious Rijíka. It is supposed to have been in what was afterwards known as the country of Kurukshetra.*

The A'ryás in the time of the oldest portions of the Collection of Laws ascribed to Manu,—which seems to be older than the rise of Buddhism, and which belongs perhaps to the seventh or sixth century preceding Christ,†—had considerably extended them-

with the *Suṣhoma*; the *Triṣhṭáma*, the *Rasá*, the *Sweti*, and the *Kubhá* (associated with the Sindhu); and the *Gomatí* and the *Krumu*. The *Rasá*, several times alluded to in the Vedas, the *Kubhá*, the *Anitabhá*, the *Krumu*, and the *Sarayu* are mentioned by Shyáváshva in the hymn following that in which he mentions the Yamuná. Ṛig-Veda, 4th asht. 3rd adh. 12th v.

* 7th asht. 2nd adh. 5th varga.

† Professor Lassen places Manu in the times preceding Buddha, on the ground of the fact that the god *Shiva*, mentioned in the Buddhist Sútras, does not appear in Manu, while of the southern nations of India, only the *Odra*, the *Draviḍa* [both on the east of the peninsula] and the *A'vantya* [that of Ujjayiní] and *Sátvata* [that of the Sátpuḍa] are mentioned by him. (chap. x.) This argument holds undoubtedly as to certain portions of Manu; but others of them may be supposed to be of a later date. Heretics are sometimes mentioned by Manu in such a keen way as to to make us believe that they had an organization hostile to that of the Bráhmans, such as first appeared in that of the Buddhists. Female devotees, unknown to Bráhmanism, and said by Kullúka Bhaṭṭa, the commentator, to belong to the

selves beyond the territory of the Indus. They were then, notwithstanding, still principally north of the Vindhya range of Mountains. "As far as the eastern, and as far as the western oceans, between the two mountains [Himavat and Vindhya] just mentioned lies the tract which the wise men have denominatied, *A'ryávarta* [the abode of the *A'ryás.*]* Included in this general region of *A'ryávarta,* but not in what we have already noticed as the *Brahmávarta,* was the region of the *Brahmarṣhi,* comprehending Kurukshetra, Matsya, Pánchál, and Shúrasena;† while the country which lies between Himavat and the Vindhya, to the east of Vinashana, and to the west, of Prayága [the junction of the Ganges and Yamuná,] was distinguished as the *Madhyadesha,* or middle country.‡ We have thus brought to notice four distinct, but advancing, settlements of the *A'ryás* in northern India, in addition to the original one

"Buddhists, etc.," are alluded to (Manu viii. 363). The reference to the *Chinas* (x. 44) would lead us to infer that portions of the work were formed after the origination of the dynasty of *Tsin* (B. C. 260) taking its name perhaps, however, from an olden tribe; and that to the *Yavanas* (ibid,) that the same portions were written subsequent to the advent of the Greeks to the north of India. It is not to be thought that the ancient Indians, who seem to have known but little of their neighbours, knew any thing of the Ionians in the ancient Grecian settlements to the west. The Code ascribed to Manu is far from being, what it professes to be, a homogeneous and monochronous work. The Hon. Mountstuart Elphinstone (History of India, p. 11.) justly says "that a code is never the work of a single age."

* Manu, ii. 22. † Manu, ii. 19. ‡ Manu, ii. 21.

on the affluents of the Indus. It would much exceed the objects and limits of this lecture, were I to attempt to trace their progress southward. Referring to the constituency of my present audience, however, I would remark that the city of *Ayodhá* (Oude) which they founded on the banks of the Sarayu, and which has become so famous by the mythical poem of the Rámáyaṇa, was probably, as the seat of the "fighting-men,"* a designation not unknown to the inhabitants of the original trans-Indian Airya; † though it is not to be wondered at that the Indians in their secondary settlements in this country, looking to the sublime and impassable mountain barriers to the north (which they assigned as the seat of their gods) should have begun to imagine that they had been, from the beginning, the inhabitants of that country, and should have altogether lost sight of their emigration from a distant land. The A'ryás probably first became known to the south of the Narmadá by the foundation of mission and mercantile establishments;‡ and, afterwards, by emigration and conquest. The Páṇḍya, if not the Chera and Chola Kingdoms, in the South of India, originated with A'ryan colonists; and, as suggested by Professor

* From the root *Yudh*, to fight.

† The word is exemplified in the Zend açpay*ayodha*, subduers of horses. See references in Vendidád of Dr. Brokhaus, p. 386.

‡ They do not seem, in the first instance, to have acted on an aggressive system of preaching in their early missions, like the Buddhists of after times, but on the attractive system of founding *Tírthas*, or religious establishments at "holy places."

Lassen, the designation of the first of these kingdoms may have arisen from a dominant "white people." The Sinhas,—from their capital *Sinhapur* (now "Sihor" near Ghogho),*—established their power on the western coasts of India, conquered the island of Lanká called from themselves *Sinhaladwípa*,† and extended their authority to several places in the eastern seas.‡ The A'ryás were so predominant in the Mahárásht̩ra, or Maráthá country, about the Christian era and the subsequent centuries, that, as distinguished from its proximate provinces, it was called *Ariaké*, the Land of the A'ryás, as by Ptolemy, the geographer of the second century, A. D., and by the navigator Arrian, thought to be his contemporary.§ A'ryá, (in the form A'ryer) is in consequence of this fact the name of a Maráthá among the Canarese of the present day, and among the Mángs a degraded tribe in the Southern Maráthá Country.‖ The *Pándhar*, or true "white"

* See Second Memoir, by the author, on the Cave Inscriptions, etc. of Western India, in vol. iv. of Journal of B. B. R. Royal Asiatic Society.

† The isle of the Sinhas.

‡ Colonel LeGrand Jacob, in an interesting Address before the Bombay Geographical Society, lately directed attention to the researches of the learned Mr. Friederich of Batavia into the Indian settlements in the Eastern seas.

§ Ptol. Geog. lib. vii. (edit. Bert. p. 198.) For the boundaries of Ariaké, as stated by Arrian, see Vincent's Periplus, vol. ii. pp. 397, 428-438. Neither Arrian nor his commentator seems to have understood the meaning of the designation Ariaké.

‖ See Máng Vocabulary in the Bombay Government Selections on Kolápur, p. 149.

still professes to be the municipality in the Maráthá villages, as the natives here present well know, though they may not yet have thought of the origin of the designation. Of the Dasyas mentioned often in the Vedas in contrast with the A'ryás, no such traces can be found, though they are once or twice mentioned by Manu.* The word *dás,* derived from *dasyu,* ultimately came to signify a bondman. In this sense, it has its analogue in our word *slave,* derived from the *Slavi* people, so many of whom have become serfs in the modern regions of their abode. Some of the names of the Dasyus and other enemies of the Aryan race mentioned in the Vedas seem to have been of Aryan origin; but we see, from the non-Sanskrit elements in the Indian languages, that they must have belonged principally to various immigrations of the Scythian or Turanian family of the human race. The more marked Turanians in Gujarát, and other provinces contiguous to us, are still denominated the *Káli Prajá,*† or black population, as distinguished from those of lighter shade, in whom Aryan blood is to a greater or less extent found.

The A'ryás in the times of the Vedas were principally a pastoral, though to a certain extent an agricultural, people.‡ Their flocks and herds, and their sheep,

* Manu, x. 32, 45.

† Vulgarly corrupted into *Parej* in Gujarát.

‡ I have marked off all the passages of the Ṛig-Veda in which the statements made in this paragraph are founded; but as they are numerous, and no critical matter is dependent on them, I do not here insert them.

goats, cows, buffaloes, horses, camels, and teams of oxen, with the hump on their shoulders, are frequently mentioned, and made the subjects of supplication and thanksgiving both to gods and men. A daughter among them in the earliest times was designated *duhiṭṛi*, or milkmaid; and a *Gopa* and *Gopál*, or keeper of cattle, among them, came to mean a protector in general, no doubt from the owners or keepers of cows having great importance in the community.* Many expressions formed from a pastoral life have got an extended generic meaning in their language.† That they were not, however, merely a nomadic people is very evident. As well as their enemies, they had their villages *(grámas)* and towns *(purís)* as well as *Goshṭhas*, or cattlepens;‡ and many of the appliances, conveniences, luxuries, and vices, found in congregated masses of the human family. They knew the processes of spinning and weaving, on which

* *Duhiṭṛi*—the correspondent of the Zend *dughdhar*, the Greek θυγάτηρ, the German *tochter*, and the Celtic *deor*,—was first noticed as "milkmaid" by Lassen. Kuhn and Lassen make *pa* in the Greek πατὴρ, Latin pater, and other cognate words, to signify "protect;" but perhaps, it is more natural to make *pa* an original word for father, and to interpret *pála*, a protector, as one who acts as a father. *Pa*,—with its anagrammatic form *áp*, and with the change of the labial and sometimes of the vowel, as in *ab*, *fa*, *ib*, etc. etc,—runs through most languages. A similar remark may be made on the originality of *má*, and *am*, *im*, etc. for mother, though *máṭṛi*, quasi mátar, in Sanskrit, as shown by Dr. Max Müller, (Oxford Essays, 1856, p. 15) may mean "former" or "maker."

† See Lassen, in O. C. S. for 1852. pp. 443–444.

‡ This word is the origin of the Sindhian *goṭ* or *goṭha*, of the same meaning.

they were doubtless principally dependent for their clothing. They were not strangers to the use of iron and to the crafts of the blacksmith, coppersmith, carpenter, and other artisans. They used hatchets in felling the trees of their forests,—among which the *Ashwattha* (Ficus religiosa), the *palásha* (Butea frondosa), and various species of Acacia, seem to have been favourites,*— and they had planes for polishing the wood of their chariots. They constructed rims of iron to surround the wheels of their carts. They fabricated coats of mail, clubs, bows, arrows, javelins, swords or cleavers, and discs or coits, to carry on their warfare; to which they were sometimes called by the sound of the conch-shell. They made cups, pitchers, and long and short ladles, for use in their domestic economy and the worship of the gods. They employed professional barbers to cut off their hair. They knew how to turn the precious metals and stones to account; for they had their golden earrings, golden bowls, and jewel necklaces. They maintained their command over the useful animals. Like the ancient Egyptians, they had chariots of war from which they fought, and ordinary conveyances drawn by horses and bullocks;† and, unlike them, they had rider-bearing steeds and grooms to attend them.

* The *Khadira,* or khair tree, the Acacia from which catechu is made, and the *Shamí,* or Acacia sami, are frequently mentioned. So are the *Shálmalí,* or Bombax heptaphyllum. The ***Kusha,*** or ***dharbha,*** grass seems to have been much esteemed. It was used in sacrifices.

† ***Ratha,*** the Sanskrit for a chariot, is recognized in the Latin *rota* a wheel. A warrior is frequently called *rathaéstáo,* a stander on a chariot, in the Pársí Zend writings.

They delighted to speak of their "well-trained horses," their "masters of horses and chariots," and their "waggons" and "famous cars." Their princes, and priests, and even gods sometimes, had names and titles derived from their connexion with the equine race. They had the elephant in a state of subjection; but it is not certain that they used it for warlike purposes, as was probably done by the Aborigines in the south.* They were acquainted with the virtues of of some herbs, and made an inebriating juice of the *Somalatá* or moonplant, the acid asclepias or *Sarcostema viminalis,* which they thought an acceptable beverage both to gods and men, even for purposes of intoxication as well as exhiliration. *Ghṛita,* or clarified butter, was as agreeable to them as to their descendants; and they were not strangers to the potency of the fermented "barley bree."† They had eunuchs in their community. The daughters of vice were seen in their towns, and that, it would appear, with but a small accompaniment of shame. Venders of spirits were also tolerated by them.‡ They had "halls of justice;" and though their worship was altogether of a domestic character, they had also "halls

* Among non-domestic animals the *vṛika*, or wolf, and the *varáha*, boar, and *sinha*, lion, are frequently mentioned.

† (यव) *Yava*, the Sanskrit for barley, is recognizable in the Greek ζία, as has been frequently noticed.

‡ The drinking of spirits, according to the modern system of the Hindus, is a *Mahápátaka*, or great sin, equal to that of incest with a mother or the murder of a Bráhman. Yet they do not support this view of matters by caste discipline, except in rare cases.

of sacrifice," and "halls of oblation." Idol-shrines are not once mentioned in connexion with them. They constructed skiffs, boats, rafts, and ships. They engaged in traffic and merchandise in parts somewhat remote from their usual dwellings; and, among other articles not found in their own territories, they had noted the soft hair of the Gandhár sheep. Occasional mention is made in their hymns of the ocean, which they had probably reached by following the course of the Indus. Parties among them covetous of gain are represented as crowding the ocean in vessels on a voyage. A naval expedition to a foreign country is alluded to, as frustrated by a shipwreck. They sent ambassadors to neighbouring princes; but it does not appear that they were much addicted to the visiting of neighbouring nations. The great river of their country was probably known to the Egyptians in the days of Moses. The *Pi-Shon* the *Sindhu,* (the first syllable of the name being, I think, the Egyptian definite article, and the Kábul affluent being anciently the principal representative of the river towards the north) is mentioned, if we err not in our interpretation, as one of the rivers of paradise in the second chapter of Genesis.*

* Though I have not seen the etymological similarity of the name above alluded to hitherto referred to, I feel disposed to lay very considerable stress on it. *Pishon* is said, in the Hebrew Dictionaries, to be derived from the root פוש, to overflow. But why should the root of Pishon be sought for in the Hebrew more than those of any of the three other rivers of paradise? *Pi,* as the Egyptian article, occurs in such names as *Pi*-Hahiroth, *Pi*-Thom, *Pi*-Beseth.

Josephus, (Jud. Antiq. i. 3. 3,) and after him many of the Christian fathers, make the Pishon the Ganges; but the sources of the Ganges are too remote from the watershed of the other rivers of Eden.

There is no evidence that the A'ryás, at the time to which we now refer, possessed the art of literal writing. The Vedas are in poetry, evidently intended for recitation; and it bears the name of the *Shruti*, or what was merely *heard*. The earliest philosophical treatises of the Hindus, which we have already noticed as posterior to the Vedas, are in the form of *Sútras, threads,* or *memorial aphorisms.* The body of law of Manu, is the *Smṛiti,* or what is *remembered.* The Rámáyaṇa and Mahábháratá, the grand epic poems of the Hindus, which in their ancient form are older than the Buddhist times, were, as rightly remarked by Professor Lassen, "*handed down orally,*" "as will be unanimously admitted."* The earliest phonetic character now found

Professor Lassen (Indische Alterthumskunde, vol. i. pp. 529-530,) on geographical grounds, identifies the Pishon with the Indus, making its associate *Ḥavilah*, the *Kámpila*, of the Indians, and the *B'dolach*, rendered by Bdellium, not this article, but the more precious one of "musk," the Sanskrit *Madálaka*, or *Madáraka*.

* Professor Lassen, who has paid much attention to these works, enters, in the second volume of his Indische Alterthumskunde, into interesting explanations respecting the composition and age of the Indian Epic Poems. They speak themselves of their being recited at great ceremonial and festival occasions. A long interval occurred between their first composition and their assumption of their ultimate form. Válmiki, who appears as the contemporary of king Ráma, cannot have been the author of the Rámáyaṇa, which refers to affairs subsequent to his day, even in its oldest portions. The Mahábhárata, which is posterior to the Rámáyaṇa, claims *Vyása* as its compiler. It does not set itself forth as an original rhapsody repeated to a king, but as a repetition of such a rhapsody made at a Bráhmanical sacrifice. It tells us that of the 100,000 distichs of which it was composed, only 24,000 belong to the original composition. The quarrel of the Páṇḍavas and Kau-

in India, that of the Cave Inscriptions,—the source of the Nágarí and all its modifications, square and rounded,—is evidently derived from the Phenician and Greek alphabets; and, as it stands, it is possibly posterior to the advance on India of Alexander the Great. Another character, of a Shemitic origin, was in use in the north of India, at least in the times of the Emperor Ashoka, and of the later Bactrian kings, on whose coins it appears. This character was probably employed in the countries bordering on India to the north before the advent of the Greeks; for after this occurrence, bringing a distinct practical alphabet from the west, there could be but little occasion for its fabrication. It may have been preceded by some cuneiform species of writing, resembling those of the Assyrians, Babylonians and ancient Persians, and expressed by *likhana*, which, though signifying "writing," originally meant "engraving" or "cutting in line;" or it may have been preceded by some species of ideagraphic writing, as that of the Chinese. One of the names of a pen in Sanskrit is *aksharatúliká*, or "letter-brush," which suits the latter supposition. *Lipi*, one of the words for writing in general, is derived from a root signifying "to besmear, anoint, or paint;" and perhaps it

ravas is covered throughout it with a great accretion of other matter. Yet, the original portions of both these poems were composed while the language in which they are written was evidently a living language. They have no allusion to Buddhism, like those of later addition. They recognize Shiva as a third great god, but incline principally to Vishnu, and are thus more ancient than the period of Megasthenes,—that of Chandragupta, Sandracottus of the Greeks,—when Bráhmanism was divided between Vishnuism and Shivaism.

was employed, in the first instance, in the case of pictorial writing, even though *mashí*, or ink, derived from *mashí*, soot or lampblack, was the fluid employed in the process.* I am somewhat confirmed in this supposition by remembering that the word *Warṇa,* applied to a letter of the alphabet, originally meant "colour," and may have been applied to a primitive ideagraphic sign in the sense of "picture." The oldest numeral system of the Hindus, as found on the Indian Cave Inscriptions prior to and subsequent to the Christian era,—as I shall attempt to show at the close of this lecture,—is in part derived from the Chinese. Having made these remarks I would add, that, though the Indians have not the credit of the original invention of an alphabet, they have the peculiar credit of extending an alphabet so as to make it expressive, with an unvarying simple power, of all the sounds of their common speech. It is also certain that they very early made astronomical observations, for, as noticed by Professor Wilson they had, even in the time of the Vedas, an intercalary month for adjusting to each other the solar and lunar years. I do not think that prior to the Greeks they had any regular system of coinage. In the time of the Vedas they dealt out gold, and perhaps the other precious metals, by weight. In the times of Manu, when very small pieces of gold and silver were current, probably a stamp representing the

* Under the various forms of *mashí*,—for the sibilant letters of the word vary,—compare Molesworth's Maráthí Dictionary with Wilson's Sanskrit Dictionary.

weight was put on the pieces, as in the incipient currency of other countries.

We have already mentioned that the Vedas are in poetry. It has several *Chhandas* or measures, which are well adapted for poetical composition and expression in the Sanskrit language. Seven of these metres are sometimes jointly mentioned, as the seven mouths of the god Agni; and most of them are sometimes exemplified in the same piece of composition. The principal of them are called the *Gáyatrí*, the *Trishṭup*, and the *Jagatí*. It is not necessary that I should speak of their peculiarities at present.

The hymns of the Vedas are called *Súktas*, or Laudations.* The gods who are addressed in them, however, are more praised on account of the benefits desired from them than on account of any excellence which they are supposed to possess. The blessings desiderated in them by the worshippers seem to be almost entirely of a material kind, and are summed up in rain, to fertilize the fields; in wealth, consisting especially of flocks and herds; in children, who, it is observable, are asked without any reference to the *Shráddhas* and other funereal rites for which they have been so much desiderated in the later times of the Hindus; in health, strength, vigour, and might; and in victory and the subjugation of enemies. Some importance seems to have been attached to the Súktas in the destruction of magic or delusion (*máyá*).† One of them, which

* *Súkta* is from *su* good, and *ukta*, spoken.

† Rig-Veda, 4th asht. 2nd. adh. sukta, 8. v. 6.

occurs near the end of the last Ashṭaka of the Ṛig-Veda, seems to have been repeated as a charm, for the removal of disease from all the members of the body.*

The slightest inspection of the Vedic Hymns, may show any native of this country that the Hindu authors of posterior times,—claiming, it will be observed, a divine sanction for their productions,—entirely err, when they represent the Vedas as an emanation in their concrete form from the mouth of the god Brahmá or any other god. The Súktas bear the names in general of their own human authors, which also often occur in their composition. The allegation made in some of the philosophical treatises and other works, that these are merely the names of the Bards who were wont to recite them, is

* Rig-Veda, 8th asht., 8th adh., 21st varga. This varga, which has not yet been printed, thus commences :—

|| आक्षिभ्यां ते नासिकाभ्यां कर्णाभ्यां छुबुकादधि ||
|| यक्ष्मं शीर्षण्यं मस्तिष्काज्जिह्वाया विवृहामि ते ||

"From thine eyes, from thy nostrils, from thine ears, from thy lips, from thy brain, from thy tongue, I expel the disorder of the head."

In this way, the *Mantra* proceeds through the various members of the body. It is quite analogous to what we find in the eighth fargard of the Vendidád of the Pársís (see Author's work on the Pársí Religion pp. 318–320) relative to the expulsion, from the body, of the fiend Naçus, by ceremonial ablution. It is repeated over the Bráhmans who receive the Ṛig-Veda on the occasion of their annual purifications, particularly in the month Shrávan. Both it and the corresponding passage in the Vendidád are interesting in a philological point of view, as dealing with most of the members of the human body, mentionable and unmentionable, and calling to mind the relationship of their names in the cognate languages.

quite inadmissible in the view of the contents of these hymns. The sages invoke the Gods for their assistance in composing them, in the same way as the Greek poets invoke the assistance of the Muses in the preparation of their songs. Such passages as the following occur in them. "Indra and Agni, desirous of wealth, I consider you in my mind, as kinsmen and relations; the clear understanding you have given me, (is given) by no one else, and (so gifted) I have composed this hymn to you, intimating my wish for sustenance."* This praise, *Maruts,* is for you, (the work) of a venerable author, capable of conferring delight (by his laudations.) May the praise reach you, for the good of your persons, so that we may obtain food, strength, and long life."† This verse occurs in the same words in another Hymn.‡ "The *Gṛitsamadas* have composed this prayer, these praises Ashvins, for your exaltation: be propitiated by them, leaders of ceremonies, and come hither; that blessed with excellent descendants, we may worthily glorify you at this sacrifice."§ Many similar passages are contained in the Vedas. Inspiration, even, in the proper sense of the term, intimating a superhuman unerring guidance, is not claimed in these compositions.‖

* Ṛig-Veda, 1st asht. 7th adh. sukta 109. Wilson's Ṛig-Veda, vol. i. pp. 281. Sanskrit text, in Müller, vol. i. p. 855.

† Wilson's Ṛig-Veda, vol. ii. p. 148 ; Müller, vol. ii. p. 298.

‡ Sukta 168. 10.

§ Wilson, vol. ii. p. 310; Müller, vol. ii. p. 612.

‖ The invention, in later times, of other origins for the Vedas has in some instances assumed a very ridiculous form. It is said (Vishnu

On examining the composition of the Vedas and other Sanskrit works, we at once see that they are in a language rightly described by our own venerable Maráthí lexicographer, as one of "vigor and elegance and majesty;"* and that the relations of this language to our own tongue are of a very interesting and intimate character. Both in grammar and vocables, it is closely connected with the Greek, Latin, Germanic, Celtic, and other European languages, which by philologers are all classed with it

Purána iii. 5) that Vaishampáyana, a pupil of Vyása, their reputed compiler, having called upon his disciples to unite with him in the performance of expiatory rites for himself, as he had been guilty of incidentally slaying his sister's son, one of them, Yádnyavalkya, refused to comply with the wish of his preceptor. For this he was called upon by his master to part with the knowledge which he had acquired from him! He forthwith out-vomited the Yajur Veda, which the other disciples of Vaishampáyana, assuming the form of partridges (*tittiri*), picked up from the ground in its several dirtied texts! From this circumstance it has received the name of *Taittiríya Kṛishṇa Yajur Veda* or the *Taittiríya* Black Yajur Veda. (The term Taittiríya, says Professor Wilson, after Colebrooke, is more rationally accounted for in the Anukramaní or Index of the Black Yajush. It is there said that Vaishampáyana taught it to Yaska, who taught it to Tittiri, who also became a teacher.) The white Yajush is said in the Vishnu Purána to have been revealed to Yádnyavalkya (the Bráhmana who had emptied his stomach) by the Sun in the form of a *Vaja*, or horse. The Konkanasth Bráhmans thus explain the origin of the name *Vájasaneya*, given to this form of the Yajur Veda (referred to in a note, p. 15 of this lecture):—वाजाः अश्वाः सनाः सटाः तेषु स्थित्वा वेदो अधीतः तेन वाजसनेय इत्युच्यते, *vájá*, horses; *sana*, manes:—seated upon them he [Yádnyavalkya, joined to the chariot of the Sun] learned the Veda, whence it is called the *Vájasaneya*.

* Preface to Molesworth's Maráthí Dictionary.

in the same family of languages, denominated the Indo-Teutonic.* The inference is unavoidable, and it is admitted by every philologer of the present day, that the A'ryás and ourselves have sprung from the same original stock. Dr. Max Müller, the learned editor of the Ṛig-Veda, thus expresses his deep conviction on this matter. "It is hardly possible to look at the evidence hitherto collected [of the intimate relation of the Indo-Teutonic family of languages] without feeling that these words are the fragments of a real language, once spoken by a united race, at a time which the historian has lately hardly ventured to realize, except on the authority of the sacred writings of the Jews. Yet, here we have in our hands the relics of that distant time."† The more the correspondence of the Sanskrit language with our own European languages is made a matter of study, the more emphatic

* See, especially, Bopp's Comparative Grammar, translated by Professor Eastwick; Eichoff's Parallèle des Langues de l' Europe et de l' Inde; and an article by A. Kuhn, entitled Zur ältesten Geschichte der Indo-Germanischen Völker in Weber's "Indische Studien," vol. ii., pp. 321-363.

† Oxford Essays, 1856, p. 30. Though this observation is made with special reference to the Indo-Teutonic languages, it is in a measure applicable to the connexion of this family with the Shemitic, and Hamitic or Turanian families. Those of us who have been engaged in the work of biblical translation in India have noticed a relationship between many Hebrew and Sanskrit words, yet but very partially brought to public notice, notwithstanding the labours of Gesenius, Rödiger, Nork, Kaiser, and others, in this department of philology. We have also noticed obvious connexions between the Sanskrit and Scythian elements of the Indian, and, to a certain extent, of the African languages.

will this remark be felt to be. Overlooking all matters connected with the composition and treatment of words in declension, comparison, conjugation, and so forth, which have been particularly illustrated by Bopp, we find hundreds of words,—connected with mythical deities, the heavenly bodies, and geographical denominations; with the material elements; with the changes of days, months, seasons, and years; with the members of our own bodies and our mental and corporeal functions; with the constitution of our families, the designation of our relatives, and our social subordination; with the names and parts of plants and animals; with our houses, villages and towns; with occupations and arts, and their utensils and instruments; with religious rites and services; with qualities and their attributes; and with motions, actions, and motives, and their effects and results,—all evidently the same in their origin and to a great extent in their utterance, even to the present day. The A′ryás and ourselves, it is hence obvious, are cousins in the human family. A body of the same people, travelling to the south, came to India, by the mountainous passes leading to the Indus, probably following their sheep and goats, and acquired dominion over the Turanian peoples, the Dasyus, that had got to the climes of the sun before them and had become in consequence somewhat darkened in their skin. Another body of the same people wandered to the far west, and, after being domiciled and blessed there, have come to India, with their ships, and with their goods, three thousand years later, and acquired dominion over the representatives of both A′ryás and Dasyus. What has taken place since the commencement of the British Government in India is only a reunion, to a certain extent, of the members of the same great family. That that reunion is not more intimate than it is, is solely owing to CASTE; respecting which I am certain I do not go beyond the convictions and the sympathies of either of the elements of this meeting, European or native, when I characterize it as the offspring of pride and deceit; as the mainspring of hatred, division, alienation, and tyranny, in this great, but, alas! still darkened land; as the curse of India, for many generations; as the unreasonable and fanatical institution, which under the grossest misrepresentation and delusion, —testified against by the full and steady toleration of the British government in India, and by the fair and open and peaceful methods of propagating religion, ever here resorted to by the Christian Church, trusting solely for its expansion to the word of God,—has professed to unfold its banners, now covered with blood and pollution, and which, in the sight of God and man, is, indeed, in this country at least, the grand *bdelugma*, "the abomination of desolation."

And this leads me to mention the interesting fact, on which I would wish specially to dwell in this lecture, that Caste is not to be found as an institution existing among the ancient Indians, during the times of the Vedas properly so-called. The *Purusha Súkta*, or Hymn of the Primeval Male, found near the end of the last Ashṭaka of the Ṛig-Veda,* in which a system

* It is also given, at least substantially, in the Vájasneyí Sanhitá of the Yajur Veda, xxxi. 1-16, and in the Atharva Veda, xix. 6. For the different readings in the three Vedas in which it occurs, see the

of Caste is first mentioned in a very obscure and undeveloped manner, is, as is evident both from its diction and pantheistic sentiments, no genuine portion of the ancient Vedas, though it would appear to have existed and attracted notice in the age of the laws fictionally ascribed to Manu. It is declared by every European orientalist capable of forming a judgment in the case to be only a late addition to the Vedas. The support which even it gives to the system of caste is of a very limited character. The passage in it which approximates the subject is the following :—"When they produced Purusha [perhaps equivalent to "when Purusha was produced"] into how many portions did they separate him? What was his mouth? What were his arms? What were pronounced his thighs and feet? The Bráhman was his mouth; the Rájanya (prince) was made his arms; the Vaishya was his thighs; and the Shúdra sprang from his feet."* This occurs in a com-

Original Sanskrit Texts, part first, pp. 8-9, of Dr. John Muir, a work, promising to be singularly useful to Indian students, which has just come into my hands as I have been making up this sheet for the press.

* The original of this passage, I subjoin, as given in the manuscripts of the Ṛig-Veda to which I have access in Bombay, and which agree with the transcript of B·urnouf. यत् पुरुषं व्यदधुः कतिधा व्यकल्पयन् मुखं किमस्य कौ बाहू का उरू पादा उच्येते ॥ ब्राह्मणोऽस्य मुखमासीद् बाहू राजन्यः कृतः उरू तदस्य यद्वैश्यः पद्भ्यां शूद्रो अजायत॥ The reader, acquainted with Sanskrit, must see that this diction is much more modern than that of the original portions of the Vedas. There are a few more hymns besides that of the Purusha Súkta, such as those treating of *A'tmá* and *Paramátmá* the Supreme Spirit, which are manifestly inter-

position which is both metaphysical and figurative; and it probably expresses an idea originally of this character: —The Bráhman, as the expositor of the will of God, conceived of as an enormous male, and the recipient of the gifts and offerings made to the divinities, was the mouth of this male; the *Rájanya*, the prince or warrior, the instrument of offence and defence, was the arms of this male; the *Vaishya*, as the cultivator of the soil and the original possessor of its wealth, was the thighs of this male; and the Shúdra, or slave, as the lowest member of the body social, was the feet of this male. All this is clearly metaphysical and metaphorical, though afterwards it was viewed as historical and dogmatic. In looking at the genuine portions of the Vedas, we ascertain the following facts, from which we draw the inference that caste did not exist in the time of the Vedas.

1. The Bráhmans are represented in the Vedas merely as a profession, and not as a caste. Not a word is said in these writings about their origin as diverse from that of other members of the human family. They ask no privileges on account of original dignity or status. They are in the Vedas merely a class of priests, officiating at sacrifices and other religious services, along with other specified classes of priests. The following are instances of the ways in which they are there mentioned. "The chaunters chaunt thee, Shatakratu [a name of Indra], the reciters of the Ṛichas praise thee, who are worthy of praise;

polations in the Veda, or which, at any rate, belong to much later times than those of the early *Súktas*.

the BRAHMA'ṆAS raise thee aloft like a bamboo pole."* "Thine, Agni, is the office of the *Hotṛi*, of the *Potṛi*, of the *Ṛitwij*, of the *Neshṭṛí;* thou art the *Agnídhṛa* of the devout; thine is the function of the *Prashástṛi;* thou art the *Adhwaryu* and the BRAHMA'; and the householder in our dwelling."† Here are eight kinds of priests mentioned, of whom the Brahmá, or Bráhmaṇa, is the last. According to some authorities, altogether sixteen kinds of priests shared in the portions of the offerings on great occasions.‡ It must have been in times later than those of the oldest portions of the Vedas that the word Brahmá, or Bráhmaṇa came to be used in the exclusive sense of god-born priest. It is not difficult, indeed, to trace the progress of the Bráhman from his Vedic profession to his subsequent position as maintained by Caste. From his peculiar position at sacrifices in the time of the Vedas, he was often their conductor, the *purohita*, or foreman, for this is the literal meaning of the word. This honour he shared only with others in the first instance, many of whom, as Vishvámitra and his school, belonged to the royal race. Agni, the god of fire was the *purohita* of the gods in the sky;§ and it was meritorious

* See Text in Müller's Ṛig-Veda, vol. i. p. 127. Professor Wilson (Ṛig-Veda, vol. i. p. 24.) reads Bráhmaṇas. In the original here, the word is Brahmáṇaḥ, the plural of Brahmá, which, as Dr. Roth has suggested, may mean the utterers of prayer. Brahmá is from Brahma (neuter), prayer.

† Wilson's Ṛig-Veda, vol. ii. p. 209, with the change of Brahmá for its equivalent Bráhmaṇ as in the text (Müller, vol. ii. p. 416.)

‡ See note in Wilson, ut sup., where the authorities are quoted and illustrated.

§ Ṛig-Veda i. 1. 1. et in mult. loc.

for kings to have a *Brahmá,* or *Bráhmaṇa* as his representative on earth. The office of the Purohita and Brahmá became hereditary; and the Brahmá, as resident in the houses of the great, became of growing consequence, especially in connexion with the anointing of kings and their horse-sacrifices, on which they counted much for conquest and progeny. His study and learning gradually increased his influence; and he was constituted an adviser and counsellor. His supposed peculiar access to the gods gave him a peculiar sanctity. He became a legislator; and in this capacity he soon made himself a god-upon-earth. Such an exaltation of a human mediator has often, to a certain extent, been witnessed in other countries besides India.

2. The writers of the Vedas, who are denominated *Ṛishis,* or inditers, and who were doubtless in a religious point of view the highest parties in the Aryan community,* call for support and countenance solely on account of their occupation and doings. Though these occupations may have been in some cases hereditary, they were not confined to one class of the Indian people. They were at least from both the kingly and the priestly classes of the population. Vishvámitra, to whom many of the Hymns of the Vedas are ascribed,† and who in the Vishnu Puráṇa,—

* The phrase, "As the Rishi among the Vipras" (rendered, in the genitive plural, by मेधाविनां "the intelligent," by the commentator Mádhaváchárya) occurs in the Sáma Veda. Author's MS. of Mádhava's commentary, part 2nd. fol. 38. Vipra is now a synonym of Bráhman. It is rendered by मेधावि, "intelligent," in the commentary on the Ṛig by Sáyaṇa.

† E. g. Ṛig-Veda, Müller, ii. p. 932, et. seq.

one of the most important legendary and traditional treatises,—is represented as one of the seven original Ṛishis of the present system of things,* was, as is admitted by all kinds of Hindu authorities, originally a *Rajarṣhi*, or a ṛishi from the rájás, though said to be elevated to the *Brahmarṣhi*, or Bráhman, grade of ṛiṣhis, for his talents, acquirements, and observances. Jamadagni, who is mentioned also in the Veda, as a Ṛiṣhí,†—

* Vasiṣhṭha, Kashyapa, Atri, Jamadagni, Gautama, Vishvámitra, and Bharadvája are the seven Ṛishis, according to Wilson's Vishnu Purána, p. 264. Other lists of the great ṛiṣhis, are given with variants in Manu, and the Puráṇas, etc. For the age of the Puráṇas,—which are all posterior to the revival of Bráhmanism after the destruction of Buddhism,—see appendix to the Notes of Colonel Sykes on Ancient India.

† "Vishvámitra is a remarkable person in the traditions of the Hindu religion : according to the historical and *Pauráṇik* authorities, he was originally a member of the *Kshatriya*, or royal and military caste, and himself for sometime a monarch : he was descended from *Kusha*, of the lunar race, and was the ancestor of many royal and saintly personages, who, with himself were called after their common ancestor, *Kushikas* or *Kaushikas*: by the force of his austerities [sic scribunt Brachmanes], he compelled Brahmá to admit him into the *Brahmanical* order, into which he sought admission in order to be placed upon a level with Vasiṣhṭha, with whom he had quarrelled: his descent, and the circumstances of his dispute with Vasiṣhṭha, are told, with some variation, in the *Rámáyaṇa*, (ch. li.—lxv. Schlegel's edition,) in the *Máhábharata*, *Váyu*, *Vishnu*, and *Bhágavata* and other Puráṇas : the details of the Rámáyaṇa are most ample : the texts of the *Ṛig-Veda* intimate a general conformity with those of the *Puráṇas* as to the family designation of *Vishvámitra*, and to occasional disagreements from Vasiṣhṭha, originating, apparently, in their respective patronage of hostile princes: according, however, to their heroic poems, the Puráṇas, and various poems and plays, these two saints were on very amicable terms in their relations to the

and who, in the later Hindu legends, is the father of the Avatára Parashuráma, is represented as the nephew of Vishvámitra. From both Vishvámitra and Jamadagni, numerous tribes of Bráhmans of mixed blood, according to the legends, claim descent. Many of the Vedic hymns are by authors said to be either of the princely class, or to have been raised from it to the priestly class.*

royal family of *Ayodhyá*, or to king *Dasharatha*, and his son *Ráma*." Wilson's Ṛig-Veda, ii. pp. 318-319. Neither the chronology nor the geography of the authorities last mentioned is of much consequence in reference to the Ṛiṣhis, who are handed about by the traditionists ad libitum, both in reference to time and place.

* Mr. Colebrooke, long ago, noticed the authorship of certain hymns of the Ṛig-Veda as belonging to royal authors, such as Mándhátṛi, son of Yuvanáshva; Shivi, son of Ushínara; Vasumanas, son of Rohidáshva; and Pratardana, son of Divodása. Other hymns of the same Veda are attributed to several of the sons of Vishvámitra as Madhuchhanda, Rishabha, and Reṇu; to Ambaríṣha; to Bharata, the father of Devashrava; to Medhátithi; to Nábhága; to Rahugaṇa; to Vatsapriya, the son of Bhálandana; to Parúruva, of the Lunar race of kings; to Vena; to Sudása; to Gṛitsamada, the son of Shunahotra, but who afterwards became the son of Shunaka; to Devápí and Shantanu; and to other princely authors. A few of the hymns of the Ṛig-Veda are even ascribed to females, real or imaginary, as Shachí, the daughter of Pulomana; Shraddhá, the daughter of Káma; Gorivítí, the daughter of Sakti; and Vák, the daughter of Abhriṇa.

On various *gottras*, or families, of Bráhmans mixed with, or derived from, the regal blood, see legendary notices in Wilson's Vishnu Puráṇa, pp. 369, 405, 448, 457, 454, etc.

Dr. John Muir, in his "Original Sanskrit Texts," pp. 44-56, has given a series of "passages sufficient to prove that according to the traditions received by the compilers of the ancient legendary history of India, (traditions so general and undisputed as to prevail over even their strong hierarchical prepossessions,) Bráhmans and Kshatriyas

3. The Ṛiṣhis and priests received in marriage the daughters of other classes of the community. The Bráhmans of the present day are well aware of this fact; but, in deference to their later Shástras, they maintain that such marriages were mere indulgences, and confined to the assumption of one wife of each of the higher classes, in addition to those of Bráhmanical rank. But what will they make of the following story, related in the Níti-Manjarí, of Kakshívat, the author of several Súktas in the Ṛig-Veda, whose mother, Ushik,—it is to be noted,—was the reputed daughter of king Anga's slave? "Kakshívat having finished his course of study, and taken leave of his preceptor, was journeying homeward, when night came on, and he fell asleep by the road-side: early in the morning Rájá Swanaya, the son of Bhávayavya, attended by his retinue, came to the spot, and disturbed the Bráhman's slumbers: upon his starting up the Rájá accosted him with great cordiality, and being struck by his personal appearance, determined, if he was of suitable rank and birth, to give him his daughters in marriage. After ascertaining his fitness, he took Kakshívat home with him, and there married him to his ten daughters, presenting him at the same time with a hundred nishkas of gold, a hundred horses, a hundred bulls, one thousand and sixty cows, and eleven chariots, one for each of

were, at least in many cases, originally descended from one and the same stock." Some of the cases referred to by Dr. Muir are the same as those of the parties mentioned in the first paragraph of this note. The historical inference ought not to be pressed beyond the bounds indicated by Dr. M.

his wives and one for himself, each drawn by four horses." Kakshívat himself, in the Veda, thus celebrates the liberality of his father-in-law:—"From which generous prince soliciting (my acceptance) I, Kakshívat, unhesitatingly accepted a hundred nishkas, a hundred vigorous steeds, and a hundred bulls, whereby he has spread his imperishable fame through heaven.* Ten chariots drawn by bay steeds, and carrying my wives, stood near me given by Swanaya; and a thousand and sixty cows followed. Forty bay horses (harnessed) to the chariots, lead the procession in front of a thousand followers. The Pajras, the kinsmen of Kakshívat, rub down the high-spirited steeds, decorated with golden trappings."† It does not appear that Kakshívat had any wives of his own class. The supply which he had from the chief was more than sufficient. Other instances of Ṛishis

* Those presents, and those which follow, are probably mentioned without much exaggeration, and seem to be liberal enough; but what are they compared with those ascribed to the kings in after times? King Bharata, according to the Anuvansha, quoted by Colebrooke (Mis. Essays, i. 42. et seq.) distributed at his consecration one hundred and seven thousand millions of black elephants with white tusks and golden coverings! Each of a thousand Bráhmans, too, received a thousand million cows as his share, better even than the gods in heaven, for the horse-sacrifice to them consisted only of seventy-eight horses burnt at the Yamuná and fifty-five at the Ganges in Vṛitraghna. According to the Rámáyaṇa, Dasharatha, at his *Ashvamedha*, gave the whole earth to the Bráhmans; but being unable to protect it, they modestly declined the present, and received in compensation a hundred thousand cows, ten times ten millions of gold-pieces, and four times this number of silver-pieces.

† Wilson's Ṛig-Veda, vol. ii. p. 14, 17-18.

and priests marrying the daughters of kings are often alluded to.*

4. The term *Kshatriya,* applied by the Shástras, or Law Books, to the second or warrior class in the Hindu community, is used in the Vedas only as a denominative of a party possessed of *kshatra,* or power. In this sense it is applied to the gods, as to Indra and Varuṇa. In the Vedas, the word *Kshetrapati,* the "owner of a field," is the name of a person possessed of landed property; and the name *Kshatrapati,* "the possessor of power," seems to have been applicable to any party exercising authority of any kind or extent. *Khsatriya* is the equivalent of *Kshatrapati.* *Kshatra* corresponds, as noticed by Lassen, with the Zend *khsathra,* which also means imperium, agreeing with the Greek κράτος, and etymologically referring to the attribute of bodily strength. Synonyms of Kshatriya, were *Vishaspati* or *Vishámpati,* a master of the people or village community ; *Raj,* the equivalent of the Latin *Rex,* a king; and *Rajanya,* a prince, the derivative of *Raj.* The kings and chiefs of the A'ryás are often praised by the Ṛishis in the Vedas; but not a word is there uttered about their emanation by birth from the arms of the Godhead. It is a great fact, as noticed by Professor Wilson and others, that "There are [in the Vedas] indications of *Rájás* hostile to the ritual who would not therefore have belonged to the recognized military order."† In the Mahábhárata,

* As those of Chyavana with Sukanya, the daughter of Sharyáti, and Jamadagni with Reṇuká, the daughter of Reṇu.

† Preface to vol. ii. of Ṛig-Veda, p. xv.

the kingly Kurus and Panchálas proceed in their senatorial deliberations without the advice of the Bráhmans, so necessary to princes according to the code of Manu.

5. In the time of the Vedas, *visha* (related to *vesha*, a house) generally meant people in general; and *Vaishya*, its adjective, was afterwards applied to a householder or to what belonged to an individual of the common people. The Latin *vicus* and the Greek οἶκος are the correspondents of *vesha*.* *Visha*, if applied, sometimes, to the pastoral, the agricultural, and the other industrial classes of the community, had reference only to their immediate occupations, without giving them any monopoly of these occupations. In an address to the Ashvins in the Ṛig-Veda, we find the general interests of the community, of the worshipper, or of the institutor of the sacrifice, thus referred to—"Favour the prayer *(brahma)*, favour the service; kill the Rakshasas, drive away the evil;......favour the power *(khatra)* and favour the manly-strength; ...... favour the cow (*dhenu*, the representative of property); and favour the people (or house, *visha*)."† Interests here

* *Visha*, was pointed out by Kuhn and Lassen as having this relationship. It occurs in the names of many of our own towns, as Green*wich*, Wool*wich*, etc., as indicated by Dr. Müller. As noticed by the antiquarian historians now mentioned, it has bẹen preserved in the Lithuanish *wiêszpatis*, lord of the manor. *Pati* is recognizable in the Greek δεσπότης. *Dama*, corresponding with the Latin *domus*, is used in Sanskrit for a single house or home.

† This passage, which occurs in the Ṛig-Veda, 6th. asht. 3rd. adh. 16th. varg., is a very important one. The text, omitting repetitive clauses, runs thus:—ब्रह्म जिन्वतमुत जिन्वतं धियो हतं रक्षांसि सेधतममीवाः...... क्षत्रं जिन्वतमुत जिन्वतं नॄन्हतं......धेनूर्जिन्वतमुत जिन्वतं विशोह. (M. S. Ṛig-Veda, of B. B. Royal Asiatic Society). In the Pada, the words are

occupy the ground which in later times belonged to particular castes. The unity of the whole immigrant race continued marked by the patronymic name A'rya,

thus separated ब्रह्म । जिन्वतं । उत । जिन्वतं । धियः । हतं । रक्षांसि । सेधतं । अमीवाः । ...... नृन॰ धेनूः । विशः ।, the word जिन्वतं being to be supplied after each of the last three words, according to the system of notation used. (Author's MS. of Pada of Ṛ. V.) Sáyaṇa Achárya, the commentator, under the caste feeling of later times, identifies *brahma* (prayer) with *Bráhmaṇa* (the man-that-prays, and *kshatra* (power) with *Kshatriya*, the party-exercising-power, and *dhenú*, the cow, and *visha*, the people, with the *Vaishya*, the party-belonging-to-the-people. This interpretation is not to be wondered at; but it is erroneous. The *mantra* referred to is a favourite one with the Bráhmans; and, both as in the Ṛig-Veda and as in an expanded form, it is much used in their more solemn and secret services, and this in such a way as to show that originally it dealt with interests and not with castes. It occurs in this enlarged form at the commencement of the Taittiríya Bráhmaṇa of the Black Yajur Veda :—ब्रह्म सन्धत्तं तन्मे जिन्वतं । क्षत्रं॰ सन्धत्तं तन्मे जिन्वतं । इषं॰ सन्धत्तं तां मे जिन्वतं । ऊर्जं॰ सन्धत्तं तां मे जिन्वतं । रयिं॰ सन्धत्तं तां मे जिन्वतं । पुष्टिं॰ सन्धत्तं तां मे जिन्वतं । प्रजां॰ सन्धत्तं तां मे जिन्वतं । पशून् सन्धत्तं तान्मे जिन्वतं. (Author's MS.) This may be thus translated:—"Maintain the *prayer*, make-it-prosperous to me; maintain the *power*, make-it-prosperous to me; maintain the *food*, make-it-prosperous to me; maintain the *milk*, make-it-prosperous to me; maintain the *wealth*, make-it-prosperous to me; maintain the *offspring*, make-it-prosperous to me; maintain the *herd*, make-it-prosperous to me." Sáyaṇa, in his commentary on this passage identifies *brahma* with the Bráhman caste, engaged for the institutor-of-the-sacrifice. *Khatra*, he makes the authority-of-the-head-of-a district. But the other terms used he does not venture to apply to any other alleged castes. In the third mantra of the Taittiríya Bráhmaṇa, the vital-breath, sight, hearing, mind, speech, etc., are coupled with the supplicatory verbs, in the same way as *brahma*, and *khatra*, evidently showing that matters pertaining to the institution of the sacrifice are referred to throughout.

to which we have often referred. The Vaishyas, in the times of the Pándavas, according to the Mahábhárata, had considerable influence in affairs of state, as exemplified in the cases of the wise Vidur and Yuyutsu. It was only by degrees, and after the A'ryás had been settled in the great plains of India, that the Vaishyas got *special* charge of flocks and herds, and agriculture, and merchandise assigned to them, as in the name of Manu; for the time was, as we have already seen, when a cowkeeper was a chieftain in their community.

6. The Shúdras, though treated by Manu and Hindu legislation in general, as a component (though enslaved) part of the Indian community, not entitled to the second or sacramental birth, are not even once mentioned in the olden Vedas. They are first locally brought to notice, in the Mahábhárata, along with the *Abhíras,* dwelling on the banks of the Indus. The *Abhíras,* are recognized as in that position by Ptolemy, who denominates the district in which they were found *Abiria*;* and their representatives are still seen in the *A'hirs,* a class of shepherds and cultivators in Sindh, Kachh, and Káṭhiáwáḍ. There are distinct classical notices of the Shúdras in this very locality and its neighbourhood. "In historical times," says Lassen, "their name reappears in that of the town Συδρος on the lower Indus, and, what is especially worthy of notice, in that of the people Συδροι among the northern Arachosians.† Thus their existence as a distinct nation is es-

* Ptol. Geo. lib. vii. p. 102. edit. Bert.

† Ptol. vii. 1. 61. vi. 20. 3. They are also mentioned by Dionys. Perieg. v. 1142, under the name Σκόδροι, in which passage other mis-

tablished in the neighbourhood of the Indus, that is to say, in the region in which, in the oldest time, the the Aryan Indians dwelt. They [the Aryans] probably conquered these earlier inhabitants; and it becomes manifest from this circumstance, that it was from the conquest of the Aborigines in the interior part of the country, that afterwards, the name [Shúdra] was extended to the whole servile caste. This name cannot be derived from the Sanskrit; and it is to be presumed that the right spelling should be *Súdra*. If this be correct, it must be sounded *Húdra* in old Persian; and this is confirmed by the statement of Megasthenes, that the Indian nations of the ʽΥδράκαι sent auxiliaries to the Persians before the time of Alexander."* The extension of the name Shúdra to the enslaved and servile classes of the country conquered by the A′ryas, in contradistinction to the more independent and more cordially hated tribes, such as the Chaṇḍálas, Ambaṣhṭhas, etc. etc., must have occurred gradually. Some of the Shúdras, and some of the more independent tribes in the interior land, I am inclined, with others, to think, may have spoken a dialect not very dissimilar to that of the A′ryás, and may have been the descendants of a prior Aryan immigration.† There seems

takes occur, as, e. g., for τῶνδε μέσοι ναιουσι Σάβαι καὶ Τοξίλοι ἄνδρες, Σκόδροι δ' ἐξείης. ἐπὶ δ' ἕσπεται ἄγρια φῦλα Πευκανέων. μετὰ τοὺς δε Διωνύσου θεράποντες Γαργαρίδαι ναιουσιν. κ. τ. λ. must be read, Σίβαι, Ταξιλοι, Σόδροι, or, according to the variant reading, Σκύδροι, Σύδροι, and Γανδαρίδαι.

* Strabo xv. 1. 6. p. 687. By Steph. Byz. ʽΥδάρκαι. They are distinct from the ʼΟξυδράκαι, called in Sanskrit *Kshudraka*. Indische Alterthumkunde, vol. i. p. 799-800.

† Many of the names of the Dasyus and other enemies of the A′ryás seem to have an Aryan meaning. There are many words cur-

to have been some hesitation in the Aryan community about the actual religious position to be given to the Shúdras. In the time of the liturgical Bráhmaṇas of the Vedas, they were sometimes admitted to take part in the Aryan sacrifices.* Not long afterwards, when the conquests of the Aryans were greatly extended, and they formed a settled state of society among the affluents of the Yamuná and Ganges, they were degraded to the humiliating and painful position which they occupy in Manu, when the following ordinance (and many others of a similar character there are) was applied to them: "Let him [a Bráhman] not give advice to a Shúdra, nor what remains from his table; nor clarified butter of which part has been offered; nor let him give spiritual counsel to such a man, nor inform him of the legal expiation for his sin: surely he who declares the law to a servile man, and he who instructs

rent in the northern family of Indian languages which appear to be more cognate with the Sanskrit than immediately derived from it. This remark is not intended to oppose the belief, also confirmed by the state of the Indian languages, that most of the tribes which entered India before the A'ryás must have been of Scythian or Turanian origin. Of the Scythian immigrations, two at least, of extensive character, are marked by the differences in the Scythian words of the northern and southern families of languages.

* Roth, in Zeitschrift of the Germ. Or. Soc. vol. i. 83, and Weber's translation of the First Adhyáya of the Shatapatha-Bráhmaṇa, also in that Journal. In this Bráhmaṇa there occurs a remarkable passage respecting the call of the sacrificers, to this effect :—"If the sacrificer be a Bráhman, it is said, *Ehi*, Come! if he is a Vaishya, then it is *Agahi*, Come hither! with a Rajabandhu [a transposition of the Vaishya and Rajanya having occurred] it is, *Adrava*, Run hither! with a Shúdra it is *Adrava*, Run hither!"

him in the mode of expiating sin sinks with that very man into the hell named *Asamvṛita*."* From the reproach of this and all similar degradation of the lower classes of Indian society, the ancient Vedas are altogether free. As already said, they do not even once allude to the existence of the Shúdra.

7. In the time of the Vedas, the idea of the god Brahmá, from whose head and arms and thighs and feet the four original castes of the Hindus are held to have been derived, was neither developed nor formed. *Brahmá*, as a member of the Hindu Triad, and as the parent of the races of man, is no god whatever of the Vedas. Brahma, in the neuter gender, in the Vedic language, means prayer; and Brahmá, in the masculine, means "he-of-prayer."† *Agni*, the god of fire and sacrifice, is the *Brahmá*, the god of prayer, and the *Vṛihaspati*, *Bṛihaspati*, or *Brahmanaspati*, the lord of prayer, throughout the Ṛig-Veda.‡

* Manu viii. 417. See pamphlet by the Author on Indian Caste, at present in the press, for further information on the comparative position of the Bráhman and Shúdra.

† Dr. Roth and Professor Lassen derive *Brahma*, from बृह्, *brih*, (it is also found in the form वृह्, *vrih*), and they view it as equivalent to "make an effort, to shake." These roots, however, mean to speak, to sound, to mutter, etc., as well as to make an effort. In the sense pointed out by Dr. Roth, they may occur, as Eichoff indicates, in the Greek βριάω, to make strong, and βρίθω to be heavy. In the sense which I have ventured to allude to (and of which many Sanskrit illustrations can be produced), it is difficult to see their correlatives in the Greek, unless it be supposed to be found in βρίμω (Lat. *fremo*) to roar, mutter, complain, and its connexions.

‡ Dr. Roth thinks that all the *pati* gods are the result of reflection and of later invention.

Though he is called *Vishpati*, *Vishámpati*, and *Manasaspati*, the lord of men; *Vaishvánara*, the sovereign of all beings; and *Játavedhas* and *Vedhas Sháshwata*, the inspector of men and the constant inspector, as practically useful to man in his person and social life, and as the constant consumer of sacrifice and offerings, he is also spoken of as "the Son of Heaven and Earth," as well as their parent, and was both a derivative god and a Creator, when the early Súktas were composed.* A desire to have a separate god for prayer, besides the gods of material nature and energy, the ancient deities of the Vedas, begins to be apparent in these writings as they advance; and for this god, Agni, in his function of Brahmá, was selected. The Bráhmans ultimately recognized Brahmá as a distinctive metaphysical god, and introduced him to public notice; but, however much they themselves contemplated him, they did not succeed in thoroughly establishing his worship among the Indian people. I have heard of only a single temple being dedicated to his honour in the whole of India.† To account for his unpopularity, it is feigned, in the later Shástras, that he is labouring under a curse from the god Shiva, who even went so far as to cut off one of his heads for his immorality!‡ *Brahma* (the divine thing *Brahma*), is

* Ṛig-Veda, 3rd. Asht. 1st. adh. s. 19. † Tod's Rájásthán, vol. i. p. 774.

‡ Author's First Exposure of Hinduism, p. 42. In the 3rd ashṭ. 8th adh. and 10th varg. of the Ṛig-Veda, Agni is spoken of as having चत्वारि शृंगा, four horns. These Sáyaṇa erroneously makes the four Vedas, the collection of which did not exist when the Súktas were composed; but M. Langlois, with much probability, makes them the four sides of Agni's eastern fire-pit, in which the myth of Brahmá's four faces may have originated.

an invention of the ideal Vedánta, a system of Pantheism long posterior to the Vedas, and really designed to supersede them under the assumed name of the "Aim" or "End" of the Vedas.*

8. The doctrine, or incident, or system, of ceremonial defilement by touch, or by eating or drinking,—by which the existence of caste is particularly marked in the present social and religious life of the Hindus,—is not recognized in the Vedas in a single instance. It is impossible that it should not, in some form or other, have been alluded to in these productions, had it existed when they were formed.

Remarks of the kind now made could easily be expanded and multiplied; but these are sufficient for the purpose for which I have made them, that of proving that Caste, in the sense in which it exists in the present day, was altogether unknown to the ancient Indians, though doubtless, like other consociated peoples, they had varieties of rank and order and occupation in their community.† The discovery of this

* This is the etymological meaning of *Vedánta*, from *Veda* and *anta*.

† *A Panchakshiti*, and *panchajana* (as in a *ṛich* quoted in a following page) are occasionally mentioned in the Vedas. Sáyaṇa A'chárya, says these expressions refer to the four *varṇas* (colours or castes) and the Nishádás treated as out-casts, or to the Gandharvas, Pitṛis, Devas, Asuras, and Rákshasas, as explained in the Nirukta. But Professor Lassen, (vol. i. p. 796.) properly observes that neither of these explanations is admissible. *Kshiti*, as he remarks, is applied in the Veda to men in general and *charshaní*, its synonym, is derived from *riṣh* to plow. The *Niṣhádas* (etymologically the "settled" Aborigines, but applied to races distinct from the Aryan) were then unknown. Even when they came into notice, they remained exterior to the Aryan state. *Jana*, signifies a person; *paṇchajani*, in times later than the Veda, an assembly of five men; and *panchajanína*,

fact is the most important connected with our Vedic research. It may aid some timid souls in dealing with Caste, that heavy, and galling, and degrading yoke, which cannot too soon be voluntarily wrenched by the natives from their own necks.

Another discovery, analogous to that which I have now noticed, which has been the result of our investigation of the Vedas is, that when they were composed, the brute creation had neither in imagination nor treatment been raised to the level of man, the chief of God's works below, and alone amongst them endowed with intelligence and moral capacity, rendering him capable of knowing, loving, and consciously serving and delighting in his Creator and Preserver. The word Man is from the Sanskrit, *manu*, he that is possessed of, or excercises, मन or मनस् *(mana* or *manas*, in Latin *mens)* a *mind*.† The lower animals, are

a chief of five men. "It is probable," Lassen adds, "that the oldest social communities consisted only of five families." That *Panchakshiti* and *panchajana* signify an aggregate of five men, is evident; but what the members of the aggregation were, it is now almost impossible to declare with certainty. Megasthenes speaks of various municipal and military Pentads as existing among the Indians in his day. (Megasthenes in Cory's Ancient Fragments, p. 220, et. seq.) Many aggregations of five persons or parties are at present recognized by the Hindus. See Molesworth's Maráṭhí Dictionary under the compound of पंच. The *A'rya Varṇa* (or colour) is spoken of as a unity in Ṛig-Veda, 3rd asht. 2. 5. 9.

† *Manu*, as a generic name for Man, is sometimes used by the worshippers instead of the personal pronouns. Its early use as a name of Man by the Aryan people led them afterwards to designate by it the First Man. मन, (mind, which also appears in the form of the verb मन् to know), has preserved its original meaning better in

in the same interesting language, the *pashu*, the cattle, or beasts, viewed as the property, of man, the Latin *pecu*, *pecunia*.* Animals were used by the Indians of the Vedas in sacrifice. The *Ashvamedha*, or sacrifice of a horse, is particularly dwelt upon by them in several important Vedic hymns. The sacrifice of the bovine race was also quite familiar to them. "Agni, descendant of Bhárata," says the Ṛishi Gṛitsamada, "thou art entirely ours, when sacrificed to with pregnant cows, with barren cows, or bulls."† But the Ṛishis made these animals, thus slain in sacrifice, alive again, says the modern Hindu. For this allegation, not the least foundation is to be found in the Veda. Animals, moreover, were not merely used by the ancient Indians in sacrifice; but they were freely used for the purposes of food. With reference to this matter as exhibited in the Vedas, the learned Professor of Sanskrit in the University of Oxford, says, "No

the Sanskrit than in the Latin *mens*, and much better than in the Greek μένος (except in such compounds as εὐμενής, δυσμενής, etc.) "The μένος of the Greeks," says Mr. Gladstone in his great work on Homer (vol. i. p. 303) "becomes the Latin *mens*, so that a particular quality, and that one belonging to the πάθη rather than the ἤθη of man, comes to stand for the entire mind." The Sanskrit shows that that the Greek has been the most aberrant in this case. It is interesting to note the permanence of the original high meaning of मन, as comprehending mind, heart, conscience, consciousness, will, liking, etc. etc., among the Indian peoples. Molesworth has devoted a couple of columns in his Maráṭhí Dictionary to its explanation and illustration.

* The root of *pashu* is *pash*, to tie, to bind.

† Wilson's Ṛig-Veda, ii. 225.

horror was attached to the notion of a joint of beef in ancient days among the Hindus." He founds this remark on the figure, occurring in one of the Súktas, of Indra "cutting in pieces the limbs of Vṛitra, as of a cow."* In the third volume of his translation of the Ṛig-Veda, he thus renders two other passages of the Vedas, which establish the justice of our assertion: "Inasmuch as he has opened the doors of the cloud and has supplied the rapid courses of the waters with (additional) torrents, so when the pious have recourse to Indra for food he finds it in the haunts of the *Gaura* and *Gavaya* [two well-known Indian species of the genus Bos];" "Bestow [Indra] upon him who glorifies thee divine food, the chiefest of which is cattle." His translation is fully warranted by the text.† The ancient Indians were unquestionably beef-eaters. Nor are they to be thought cruel and unmerciful simply on this account. An ox suffers more from a day's hard labour in a cart or a plough, than from the blow, puncture, or cut of the butcher's instrument, or from a struggle with a beast of prey. The following suggestive passage, bearing on this matter, appears in the admirable volume of

* Wilson's Ṛig-Veda, vol. i. p. 165. Though the word गोर्न separated as गो: । न । in the Pada of the Veda, and manifestly expressing Cow, is used, the commentator, to avoid the mention of that now "sacred" animal, supplies the clause, as "worldly men, the carvers of *flesh*, divide here and there the limbs of *animals*." See Text, Müller, vol. i. 451.

† Ṛig-Veda 3rd asht. 6th adh. 6th varg.; 4th asht. 7th adh. 11th varg.

travels by the "African Columbus," as he has been called, Dr. Livingstone, which has just appeared. "The lion caught my shoulder as he sprang, and we both came to the ground below together. Growling horribly close to my ear, he shook me as a terrier dog does a rat. The shock produced a stupor similar to that which seems to be felt by a mouse after the first shake of the cat. It caused a sort of dreaminess, in which there was no sense of pain nor feeling of terror, though [I was] quite conscious of all that was happening. It was like what patients partially under the influence of chloroform describe, who see all the operation, but feel not the knife. This singular condition was not the result of any mental process. The shake annihilated fear, and allowed no sense of horror in looking round at the beast. This peculiar state is probably produced in all animals killed by the carnivora; and, if so, it is a merciful provision by our benevolent Creator for lessening the pain of death."* I leave the natives now present to draw their own inferences from this passage.

The maintenance by the ancient A'ryás of perfect lordship over the brute creation now referred to,—a lordship which claimed them as the servants, or supports, of man, both for labour and food,—is a presumption that the doctrine of the Metempsychosis, or transmigration of the human soul into brute and vegetable forms, had not then been propounded. Of this doctrine, indeed, no trace is to be found in the ancient hymns of the Vedas. The celestial elevation of the

* Livingstone's Travels and Researches in South Africa, p. 12.

sons of Angiras; of the Ribhus, the sons of Sudhanvan; and ultimately, of the seven Ṛishis as the stars of the constellation of the Great Bear, directly militates both against it, and against the notion of the absorption of the spirit of man into the substance of the Divinity.* The invention of the metempsychosis, in aftertimes, has had a most degrading effect on the Hindu mind. The bringing of the brutes up to the level of man has brought down man to the level of the brutes. It has driven man entirely from the apprehension of his right position in the scale of creation. It has confused, compounded, and confounded him, to his great dishonour, with beasts and birds, and reptiles, and fishes; with the lowest invertebrated animals; with the plant-like animals; and even with vegetable organisms of every species and variety. I am now an intelligent man, but soon I may be a chattering monkey; I am now a tender-hearted woman, but erelong I may be a ravening wolf; I am now a studious boy, but next year I may be a stupid buffaloe; I am now a playful girl, but after my next birth, I may be a skipping goat. That querulous crow may be my own deceased father; that hungry cat, my own departed mother; that raging bear, my quondam brother; and that crawling serpent, my late sister. This is the legitimate language of the metempsychosis. It is generally current among the people of this country; and it has brought them under the slavish fear of the lower animals, even of reptiles, which, according to the present institutes and practices of caste, but contrary to the

* Several Hymns specially addressed to the Ribhus are to be found in the 3rd ashṭaka, 7th adh. of the Ṛig-Veda.

warrant of the Veda,* they refrain from killing, even when they encroach on the habitations of man.

Other interesting discoveries, like those now adverted to, are to be made by the study of the Vedas.

The horrid rite of Satí has no sanction in the Vedas, though the Bráhmans are accustomed to quote from them a passage favourable to the burning of widows. That passage, as has been shown by Professor Wilson, who has critically investigated its import, speaks of the conservation and not of the cremation of the widow. The Bráhmanical translation, as given by Colebrooke, is, "Om! let these women, not to be widowed, good wives adorned with collyrium, holding clarified butter, consign themselves to the fire! Immortal, not childless, nor husbandless, well adorned with gems, let them pass into the fire, whose element is water."† The philological and critical translation of it is, "May these women, who are not widows, but have good husbands, draw near with oil and butter. Let those who are mothers go first to the altar, without sorrow, but decked with fine jewels." It occurs in a hymn addressed to Mṛityu, or Death, and used in the funeral services of the Ṛig-Vedí Bráhmans. The perversion made of the passage was by the change of a single syllable, the substitution of *agneḥ* for *agre*, making the clause, "Let those who are

* See the Súkta used for relief from the poison of serpents, in Ṛig-Veda 2nd asht. 5th adh. 14th-16th varg. In the second verse of this hymn, there is a reference to the destruction of serpents; and in the fourteenth, to the slaying of a *nakula*, or mungús, by a stone, in case of its failing to carry off the poison.

† Colebrooke's Miscell. Essays, p. 116.

mothers go first to the altar," read, "Let those who are mothers go into the womb of the fire." Well has Dr. Müller said, "This is perhaps the most flagrant instance of what can be done by an unscrupulous priesthood."* The passage does not refer to the bereaved widow, but to the visit of condolence to her by unbereaved female friends. The bereaved widow is thus addressed in the verse which follows it:—"Rise up, woman, come to this world of life; thou sleepest nigh unto him whose life is gone. Come to us. Thou hast thus fulfilled thy duties of a wife to the husband who once took thy hand, and made thee mother."† In this earnest call, there is a pleasing expression of affection and sympathy. The discredit of the incremation of widows is consequently not to be associated with the older forms of Hinduism. There is no instance of Satí, or precept referring to Satí, even in the Code ascribed to Manu.

I am sorry that I cannot, as now done in the case of Satí, exempt the Vedas from the direct encouragement of Man-sacrifice, or *narmedha*. In the first Ashṭaka of the Ṛig-Veda, the intended sacrifice, as in a rite, of

* Oxford Essays, 1856, p. 22. The paper on the passage by Professor Wilson is contained in the Journal of the Royal Asiatic Society, vol. xvi. p. 201, et seq.

† For the sake of my native friends, I subjoin the original of both the verses, from the 7th ashṭaka, 6th adh., 27th Varga of the Ṛig-Veda.

इमा नारीरविधवाः सुपत्नीराञ्जनेन सर्पिषा संविशंतु ॥
अनश्रवोऽनमीवाः सुरत्नारोहंतु जनयो योनिमग्रे ॥
उदीर्ष्व नार्यभिजीवलोकं गतासुमेतमुपशेष एहि ॥
हस्तग्राभस्य दिधिषोस्तवेदं पत्युर्जनित्वमभिसंबभूथ ॥

Shunashephas, the son of Ajígartta, is brought to notice in a series of hymns, which he is represented as reciting when tied to the sacrificial tree or post. The rite has more or less continued among the Indians from the time of the Vedas to the present day.*

Baby marriages, if at any time practised in the times of the Vedas, were not then imperative. The following passage is decisive on this matter. "As a virtuous maiden, growing old in the same dwelling with her parents, (claims from them her support), so come I to thee for wealth."† Woman is spoken of in the Veda, as "the light of the dwelling" of the ancient A'ryás, no unequivocal index of her importance and of the kindness of the treatment she received among them. Though the wife seems to have often had a conveyance allotted to her by them distinct from that of her husband, she

* In one of the groups of figures in the Caves of Elephanta, the comparatively modern god Shiva, in the form of Bhairava, is represented as about to sacrifice a child. The child he holds in one hand, while he has a bare sword, to strike the fatal blow, in another; a bell, to intimate the appointed moment, in a third; and a vessel, to receive the blood, in a fourth, there being altogether eight hands to the figure.

† Wilson's Ṛig-Veda, vol. ii. p. 251. There is a curious hymn addressed to the Maruts by a Ṛishi named Shyáva, or Shyávashva, priest of Rathavíti, dwelling near the mountains of the Gomatí river, with whose daughter he fell in love. This ṛishi was employed by Shashíyasí to negotiate a marriage in her behalf with Taranta, the son of Purumiḷha, the son of Vidadashva. He was successful in the enterprize in behalf of the lady, for which he was rewarded with a hundred cows. He then invoked the Maruts to aid him in getting his own love. Ṛig-Veda, 4th asht. 3rd adh., Müller, iii. 489-495. See also note in Langlois, Ṛig-Veda, pp. 37-38.

suffered from nothing like the exclusion and confinement of modern times. She was permitted to take an active part even in religious services. "This," says Professor Wilson, "is contrary to the precepts of the law, which prohibit her sharing in the celebration of any solemnity, except that of marriage, and she is on no occasion to recite Mantras, sacred or Vaidik texts.*

The course of religion established among, and practised by, the A'ryás in the time of the Vedas,—though even in those early days a course of heathenism,—was of a far more simple and intelligible character than that of the Hindus in later times. Thirty-three gods are mentioned in the Vedas. "Gods who are eleven in heaven; who are eleven on earth; and who are eleven dwelling with glory in mid-air; may ye be pleased with this. our sacrifice."† The later Hindus, by a something like a sevenfold arbitrary use of the cipher,—the origin of which I shall notice at the close of this lecture,—multiplied these gods to the inconvenient number of 330,000,000, more easily pronounced, I should say, than counted.‡.

* Wilson's Ṛig-Veda, vol. ii. 37.

† Ṛig-Veda, 2nd asht. 2nd adh. 4th varg.

येदेवासो दिव्येकादश स्थ पृथिव्यामध्येकादश स्थ ।
अप्सुक्षितो महिनैकादश स्थ ते देवासो यज्ञमिमं जुषध्वं ॥

‡ The commencement of an arbitrary use of numbers in reference to the gods is apparent even in the Ṛig-Veda itself. In the 3rd asht. 1st adh. 7th, varg., we find the following remarkable invocation, addressed to Agni:—

त्रीणि शता त्री सहस्राण्यग्निं त्रिंशच्च देवा नव चासपर्यन्।

In many passages of the Vedas, Heaven and Earth *(Dyává Pṛithiví*)* are spoken of as parent gods ;† but so, frequently, are other divinities so-called. The Triad principally introduced to notice,—by association and not by dogmatic announcement,—consists of *Indra*, our own *Ether*, the god of the air, piercing the clouds with his thunderbolt, the product of his assistant *Tvashtṛi*, to induce them to shed down their watery treasures;‡ *Varuṇa*, the *Ouranos* of the Greeks, the

"Let the three hundred, three thousand, and thirty-nine gods glorify Agni." M. Langlois (Ṛig-Veda, ii. p. 229) supposes these numbers to be thus formed.

33
303
3,003 which, when added make

3,339, agreeing with the text, but, with two additional ciphers interposed, expressed by M. Langlois by 303039.

That 33 is an element in this curious combination, is taken for granted by Sáyaṇáchárya, (Müllẹr's Ṛig-Veda, ii. p. 686), who makes it comprehend the 8 Vasavas, 11 Rudras, 12 A'dityas, 1 Indra, and 1 Prájápati. The other elements of the summation seem to have been a puzzle to that learned Bráhman. The ancient Grammarian Yáska, as noticed by Colebrooke, resolves all the gods of the Veda into three. "There are three divinities," he says, "and earth, air, and sky are their dominions; and *Agni*, *Váyu*, and *Súrya* their names." This, however, is a generalization posterior to the Vedas.

* *Pṛithiví* has no correspondent in Greek or Latin, but *dhará*, (the supported) another name of the Earth, is perhaps allied to *terra*.

† The collective gods are mentioned as their "sons" in Ṛig-Veda, 2nd asht. 5th, adh., 2nd. varga, and in other places.

‡ Indra, though not in absolute divine lordship, is certainly the correspondent of the Greek Ζεύς and Ζεύπατηρ. The latter designation is etymologically intelligible from the Sanskrit द्युपितृ (*Dyupitṛi*),

god of the encircling canopy of heaven ;* and *Agni*, the Latin *Ignis*, the Lord of Fire and Heat, and the priest, absorber, or conveyer to the other gods, of all sacrifices.† These gods have each respectively their wives, *Indráṇí*, *Varuṇání*, and *Agnayí*. Associated with Indra, and often subordinated to him, are *Váyu*, the god of the Wind ;‡ *Rudra*, not in the Vedas a name of Shiva, who was then unknown, but the god of roaring Tempests; the *Maruts*, or faint Breezes, the sons of Rudra; and *Vishṇu*, the god of the brilliant Firmament. The gods of Light, have a prominent place, as *Súra* or *Súrya*, the Sun, with various designations founded on his aspects and effects connected with the progress of the day and of months and seasons;§ *Ushas*, the Dawn,|| with the *Ashvins*, or riders,

the Father-of-the-Sky or of Heaven. *Dyu*, as a radix, means to shine. The cognate word for *Indra* in Greek, is αἰθήρ, which must have originally meant the clear or shining sky.

* The ancient Indians seems to have had most to do with Varuṇa in their moral relations, as it is to him that confession of sin is most distinctly made in the Vedas. He is in the later Hindu mythology the god of the Ocean.

† With the Sanskrit *Ulká*, a flame, corresponds the Latin *Vulcanus*.

‡ *Váyu* is from *Vá*, to, move or blow. *Váta*, another form of the word, has the Latin *Ventus*, and the Zend *Váta*, as its correspondents.

§ The Greek 'Ηώς corresponds with *ushas*. Liddell and Scott derive 'ηώς from the Sanskrit *vá* (to blow). It probably comes from *ush*, which occurs both in Sanskrit and Zend in the sense of to burn, to glow.

|| The ancient Indians, like the Greeks (e. g. Homer. iii. 276), attributed the perfection of hearing as well as seeing to the Sun ; and they sought to contemplate him as they were contemplated by him.

her precursive Rays; *Chandramas*,* or the Moon (but seldom mentioned), also a forerunner of the Dawn; and the *Vasus*, the personified solar rays. *Nakta*, or Night, herself, is a goddess.† *Yama*, the Subduer, or god of human Destiny, with *Yamí* his spouse, and *Mṛityu*, or Death, are recognized. *Shukra*,‡ the planet Venus, is mentioned in the Sáma Veda as intoxicated with the Soma juice, which has also its own god *Soma*, sometimes figuratively the Moon. *Bṛihaspati* in the Vedas, is not the planet Jupiter, but the "lord of prayer" a name of Agni, who, as already noticed by us, has also other similar names, including *Brahmá*, of the same import. *Sarasvati*, afterwards the wife of Brahmá, is the goddess of eloquence. She is associated with *Ilá* or *Iḍá*, and *Bhárati* (the Earth), goddesses of Song. The *A'paḥ*, or Waters, are personified; and the *A'ptyas* are water-goddesses. The *Vishve-Devas* are sometimes spoken of as the Collective Gods, and sometimes as special gods the Protectors of men, in both senses, I think, corresponding with the Amsháspands and Izads of the

Professor Lassen (Indische Altherthumskunde, vol. i. p. 761.) traces the Greek, Latin, Gothic, and other Indo-Germanic names of the Sun to the Sanskrit root *ṣhu* to bear, produce. The Greek Ἥλιος and the Doric Ἅλιος (from ΣαϜέλιος) seem recognizable in the Gothic *sáuil* and *sunno*, and, like *sol*, come near the Indian names.

* Masculine in Sanskrit. *Chandra*, as shown by Lassen, corresponds with the Latin *candor*, brightness. *Mas* is from *má* to measure, applied to time in the months of the year.

† *Nakta* obviously corresponds with the Latin *nox* and the Greek νύξ.

‡ Masculine in Sanskrit.

Pársís. Among remarkable personifications is *Aghá*, the goddess of Evil,* corresponding in some respects (though not with the dualistic notions of Zoroaster) with the Ahriman of the Parsis. The *Sindhu*, or river Indus, is a god, and the other Rivers of the Vedas, goddesses. The Ocean also is a divinity. The *Pitṛis*, or typical ancestors, corresponding with the Faruhars of the Pársís, are often addressed; and the *Vasus*, already referred to as the solar rays, seem, in some aspects, to be similar to them.† The *Ṛibhus* are deified men, as were afterwards the principal stars of the Great Bear.‡ But I must not here further enlarge on the Vedic divinities individually considered, though I must add that many of the principal gods of the Hindus are not even once mentioned in the Vedas, and that, consequently, they must be considered the inventions of

* See Rig-Veda, 8th aṣhṭ., 5th adh., 23rd. varg; Sáma Veda, Uttara Sanhitá, 11th prapáṭh. 3d-4th verse. Some copies, as that of the B. B. R. A. S., read *Apva* for *Aghá*, but this by a scriptive error. See the commentaries. Benfey gives *Aghá* in his text, and *apva*, in his translation, of the Sáma. The Zend for Ahriman is *aǧhro-mainyu*, the evil-minded-one.

† On the meaning of the word *Vasu*, see Benfey's Sáma-Veda, p. 166. As a domestic God Ves-ta (Ἑσ-τία) is there compared with *Vasu*.

‡ "According to the Nirukta etymology, Ṛibhu means much light, from *uru* much, and *bhá* to shine." Wilson's Ṛig-Veda, vol. i. p. 286. "*Orpheus* is the same word as the Sanskrit *Ṛibhu* or *Arbhu*, which though it is best known as the name of the three Ṛibhus [referred to above], was used [also] in the Veda as an epithet of Indra, and a name of the Sun. ...... There may have been an old poet of the name of Orpheus,—for old poets delight in solar names; but the story of Orpheus and Eurydike was neither borrowed from a real event, nor invented without provocation." Müller, in Oxford Essays, 1856, p. 79.

later times. In the Vedas we have no Shiva,—though the Bráhmans wish to find him in Rudra there mentioned,—and none of the members of his family, such as Durgá or Kálí, his spouse or spouses, and Ganesha, and Kártikeya, his sons. In the Vedas we have no Náráyaṇa; and the Vishṇu of the Vedas is not of the same character as the Vishṇu of the now reputed Triad. In the Vedas, we have no Ráma or Krishṇa, afterwards so popular as deified heroes or as the alleged incarnations of Vishṇu. In the Vedas, we miss some of the planetary, and many of the minor, deities of the Hindus.

The Vedic treatment of the gods actually recognized is peculiarly interesting, as shedding great light on the origin of polytheism aud mythology. It is, considered in a general point of view, the deification of the prominent objects, energies, agents, and phenomena of nature in their different aspects, particularly as connected with the firmament; and this by parties failing to recognize the spirituality and omnipresence of God,—of whom, probably, they had traditional impressions,—and making the various manifestations of power and glory around them the sensible exhibitions of the action of a diversity of deities. To some extent, also, it has got into the shape in which we find it by figurative and poetical description, and even personifications by gender, having, in the progress of time, been mistaken for the revelation of real living personages. It is long since the attempt was made by me to direct, in public lectures, the attention of the educated youth of this city to both these characteristics of the Vedic religion. The latter of them is illustrated, in the most beautiful and striking manner, by Dr. Max Müller in his admirable paper on "Comparative Mythology," in the Oxford Essays for 1856. I take from that valuable document only a small portion of a single paragraph. "There is, fortunately, no system of religion or mythology in the *Veda*. Names are used in one hymn as appellatives, in another as names of gods. The same god is sometimes represented as supreme, sometimes as equal, sometimes as inferior to others. The whole nature of these so-called gods is still transparent; their first conception, in many cases, clearly perceptible. There are as yet no genealogies, no settled marriages between gods and goddesses. The father is sometimes the son, the brother is the husband, and she who in one hymn is the mother, is in another the wife. As the conceptions of the poet varied, so varied the nature of these gods. Now here is the wide distance which separates the ancient poems of India from the most ancient literature of Greece, more clearly felt than when we compare the growing mythes of the Veda, with the full-grown and decayed mythes on which the poetry of Homer is founded. The Veda is the real Theogony of the Arian races, while that of Hesiod is a distorted caricature of the original image. If we want to know whether the human mind, though endowed with the natural consciousness of a divine power, is driven necessarily and inevitably [without the restriction and guidance of divine revelation] by the irresistible force of language as applied to supernatural and abstract ideas, we must read the *Veda;* and if we want to tell the Hindus what they are worshipping — mere names of natural phenomena, gradually obscured, personified, and deified—we must make them read the

Veda. It was a mistake of the early Fathers to treat the Heathen gods as demons or evil spirits, and we must take care not to commit the same error with regard to the Hindu gods. Their gods have no more right to any substantive existence than Eos or Hemera —than Nyx or Apatê. They are masks without an actor,—the creations of man, not his creators; they are nomina, not numina; names without being, not beings without names."

In the same way that the Vedas throw light on the origin of mythology, they throw light, I conceive, on the origin of the doctrine of spiritual pantheism,—a doctrine, however, which, as we have already hinted, they do not categorically contain. Individual gods mentioned in them are often spoken of by their worshippers as their all in all, as discharging the functions of the combined divinities, and as being the very objects over which they extend their sway. Thus, *Aditi,* the goddess of the Earth, is is thus addressed: "Aditi is the heaven, Aditi is the firmament, Aditi father, mother and son; Aditi is the *Vishve-Devas* (all the gods collectively); Aditi is the *Pancha-jana* (the pentads of the people) Aditi is generation; Aditi is birth."* Thus, Indra is represented as saying, "I was Manu, I am the Sun, I am the wise Rishí Kakshívan," and so forth.† Thus of the Sun, it is said, "They have denominated him Indra, Mitra, Varuṇa,

* अदितिर्द्यौरदितिरंतरिक्षमदितिर्माता स पिता स पुत्रः ॥
विश्वे देवा अदितिः पंच जना अदितिर्जातमदितिर्जनित्वं ॥
Ṛig-Veda, 1st asht. 6th adh. 16th varg.

† अहं मनुरभवं सूर्यश्चाहं कक्षीवां ऋषिरस्मि विप्रः
Ṛig-Veda, 3d asht. 6th adh. 15th varg.

Agni, and he is the celestial well-winged Garutmat, for the intelligent (Vipras) call one by many names, such as Agni, Yama, Mátarishvan."* Such identifications as these, combined with the personification and deification of material nature, would lead directly to Pantheism. What was merely figurative, in such instances, was afterwards viewed, in the progress of Hindu speculation, as actually real. What was at first only mysticism, was afterwards considered perfect philosophy.

It is possible that idols, the works of men's hands, were partially in use in the times of the Vedas, for the members of the imaginary bodies of the gods are sometimes spoken of with considerable particularity; but idols are not mentioned in connexion with the direct religious services of the A'ryás, which consisted principally in the preservation of the sacred fire, and in the offering to the gods of the Soma juice, of liquefied butter, of animal sacrifices, and of hymns recited and chaunted. When the Indians, in later times, lost sight of the subordination of the objects of their worship, and constructed artificial idols of their gods, their Aryan brethren of Bactria (the Zoroastrians),—whose ancient Hymns as, seen in the Yaçna and Yashts, etc., of the Pársís very much resemble the Hymns of the Vedas, treating often of the same gods in similar style,—raised, it is believed, a loud protest against this deterioration and corruption of worship, even treating the Hindu *Devas* as Devils, and making *Indra* himself,

* इंद्रं मित्रं वरुणमग्निमाहुरथो दिव्यः स सुपर्णो गरुत्मान् ।
एकं सद्विप्रा बहुधा वदंत्यग्निं यमं मातरिश्वानमाहुः ॥
Ṛig-Veda, 2d asht. 3d adh. 22d varg.

the Devil *Andar.** In a certain manner and degree we honour the Zoroastrians for this protest; but we, the cousins of the Aryans from the far west, raise our voice, as is well known, against the worship of both artificial and natural idols of any form or character. Even to the great luminary of the heavens, the most glorious object which presents itself to our view, we refuse to give the name of Lord, *Asura*, or *Ahura.*† We view the Sun as only the work and agent of deity, and devoutly say,

> "Infinite God, thou great unrivalled ONE!
> Whose glory makes a blot of yonder sun,
> Compared with thine, how dim his beauty seems,
> How quenched the radiance of his golden beams."

The matters now referred to I do not at present discuss in their extensive religious bearings; and here I draw to a close, though some minor matters connected with our subject, and not altogether without interest, I have failed to notice.

Our brief survey of the A'ryás on the banks of the Indus, will, I trust, not be without its use both to the

* This is the popular name of this Devil. In the Zend-Avasta, it occurs both as *Iñdra* and *Añdra.*

A very interesting paper might be written on the accordances and and antagonisms of the Veda and the Avastá. See an important contribution to their elucidation by Professor N. L. Westergaard, in the Journal of the B. B. R. A. S. No. xviii, in which, with original notices, the researches respecting them of several German orientalists are referred to.

† *Asura* is applied to the Sun and to fire in Ṛig-Veda, iii. 4. 1. 12; iv. 5. 4. 1; iii. 4. s. 1. 57. v. 78. and in other places. This in Zend is *Ahura*, rendered by Burnouf, Lord. *Ahura-Mazda* (Hormazd) means the multiscient Lord. I have no doubt, however, that *Ahura* was originally the sun, denominated as Master, as we find in Baal, Moloch, etc.

members of this energetic institution from the favoured climes of Britain, and to the numerous natives of India whom I have now the pleasure of seeing before me in this assembly. The acquisition of the Vedas gives us a veritable view of an interesting portion of the ancient world, and reveals to us the workings of the human mind under very peculiar circumstances and conditions. "India three thousand years ago," when viewed in its own social aspects, was actually better in many respects than India at the present day. India at the present day, however, is more hopeful than India three thousand years ago. India three thousand years ago was just in the infancy of error and misery, destined to attain to a fearful growth. It had lost sight of the great Creator of heaven and earth, both in its thought and worship; and was ready, both in speculation and practice, to wander farther and farther from the centre of truth, light, and love. It had no idea of a universal providence directed by an omniscient and omnipotent God; and it deified the agencies and phenomena of nature, and prostrated itself before them without the distinct recognition of their great Author. Of moral relations as connected with divine law, of which they are the correlatives, it had but a faint idea. Though it attached great importance to sacrifice, it had lost sight of its rationale, as the primitive type of acknowledged guilt on the part of man and of a great ransom from deserved punishment to be granted in the mercy of God through a great Deliverer. It had bards and priests most signally covetous of wealth and honours,—as evinced by their extravagant commendations of those who bestowed on them gifts and largesses,—and ready to put forth and enforce those claims of authority and preëminence which erelong issued in the institution of Caste. Its military rulers enslaved the nations and peoples whom they conquered, and began to exercise over them the most humiliating oppression, depriving them of religious liberty, and falling short of the full recognition of their common humanity. India, at the present day, though it is in the maturity of what, since the time of the Vedas, has been a continuous course of growing evil, has been challenged, if not arrested, in its ruinous career by wonderful providential dispensations. It has become allied, partly by its own consent, and partly by provoked conquest, with what we have already termed the most enlightened and philanthropic nation in the world. Little more than a year ago, I thus noticed, in a public discourse, the palpable benefits of this connexion. "The consequence has been the deliverance of India, with exceptional districts peculiarly situated, from violence and oppression; and the bestowment upon it of peace, law, order, and religious liberty, blessings which it never enjoyed under any of its dynasties, however remote. Britain, notwithstanding all her faults and shortcomings,—and these we have no wish either to excuse or palliate,—is in reality taking India into her kind and parental embrace, seeking to bestow upon it, by degrees, all the blessings of which she herself is in possession, or which she herself is striving to obtain. She is labouring to lighten and adjust its burdens, and to multiply its agricultural resources. She has given the whole oceans of the globe to be the quiet pathway of her commerce.

She is joining district to district, and province to province, by roads and bridges and excavations of mountain passes, and by a system of communication, by steam and lightning and land and sea and air, which its inhabitants deem miraculous. She is seeking to elevate all her tribes in the scale of humanity. She is seen, as an angel of mercy, arresting alike the hand of the infatuated orphan son kindling the funeral pyre to burn the living as well as the dead parent; the hand of the parent cruelly put forth to destroy, in the pride of tribe and caste, the unwelcome female child; and the hand of the misguided and miserable devotee seeking to extinguish his own life. She has put an end to the drink-offerings and meat-offerings of human blood and human flesh to gods and devils. She is seeking to dispense justice and judgment throughout the land, improving from time to time the instruments of her administration, many of whom, as can easily by accounted for, are but imperfect and unsuitable. The enlightenment of India, in literature, art, and science, and the facilitating the diffusion of the truth throughout its borders, have been and are now, more than ever, her anxious care."* After the occurrences of the past year,—the *annus tristis* in the annals of British India,—in which a portion of the sons of India have, with so much wickedness and cruelty, sought to destroy their great benefactors, shall I modify the language here used, and qualify the hopes which the facts here noticed awaken in our bosoms? No! Looking at affairs in their general aspects, and with a devout recognition of providential dispensations,

* Star of Bethlehem, pp. 35-36, 2d. edit.

which still point to a glorious issue, this I shall not do. The events of the past year have revealed to us, Britons, our errors in the interpretation of the social materials around us, and of our own shortcomings in connexion with the agencies with which we have to deal with them; but they have rather quickened than extinguished our benevolence and beneficence, and strengthened rather than diminished our determination to labour for the good of India as well as for the stability of the British empire in all its extent. The growing intelligence of India will henceforth, more than ever, perceive our power under God, and appreciate the blessings which we have to offer to all to whom our sway extends. The British sovereignty is still here in her mercy and compassion as well as in her majesty and compulsion. The soldier is here; and he is fighting for peace and order, and not for war and plunder. The administrator is here; and it is the common weal which he is striving to promote, and impartial justice which he is seeking to dispense. The merchant is here; and what he cannot obtain by the simple exchange of commodities, he pays for by the silver and gold of other climes. The engineer is here; and in alliance with the subtile agencies of nature framed and guided by an unerring providence, and with the cunning resources of science and art, he is devising and executing public works of inestimable utility and grandeur,—like those to which our attention was so lately directed in this place by the accomplished and able president of this institution.* The

* Allusion is here made to Mr. Berkley's interesting paper on the Bor Ghát Incline (the largest in the world,) for surmounting the Sahyádrí range of mountains.

educationist, both of the school and the press, is here; and he is dispensing that instruction in which centre all the secular resources and appliances of which the most advanced nations on the face of the globe are possessed. The missionary is here; and he is bearing tidings of love and grace from heaven, and of a full and glorious salvation, extending both to the life which now is and that which is to come, purchased by the manifested Son of God, and to be conferred on all who will believingly and heartily receive it. India to-day, I hold, is only passing through a mental and spiritual metamorphosis, destined, through the grace and power of God, to issue in its complete regeneration. The present troubles in the North-west,—the seat of the A′ryas in the times of its organized Brahmanical legislation,—are, I hope and believe, only the birth-throes of its Civilization and Christianization.

SUPPLEMENTARY NOTE ON THE ORIGIN OF THE UNITS OF THE INDIAN AND EUROPEAN NUMERALS.

[*Delivered at the close of the preceding Lecture.*]

IT is not my intention at present to enter into what may be called the literature of the various questions which have been raised relative to this interesting matter. With that literature, except as connected with Indian research, I am but partially acquainted. I confine my attention to the results of my own incidental observation, which several of my friends, to whom I have occasionally shown them, have pronounced satisfactory, and who,—like Mr. Layard on his late visit to Bombay, — have urged me to give them in some form or other to the public.

1. The first unit, *one*, occurs in the Cave-inscriptions of Western India as a single horizontal bar, of this form —. For the expression of a fractional unity it is still retained in this position, as is well known,

at least in the provinces contiguous to ourselves. It is identical with the Chinese 一 (*ye*), from which it is in all probability derived. In its cursive form it has assumed an upright position, with such a cursive head as haste, or taste in writing, may have produced. In the Maráthí current hand it appears as १. With the Arabs, who acknowledge that their alphabet was derived from India, it is ١. With the Modern Europeans, who have derived their numerals from the Arabs and Moors, it is 1.

2. The Cave form of *two* is 二, agreeing with the Chinese 二. This form is preserved also in Indian fractional notation. It is the origin of the Indian cursive two, formed thus ⅔, and appearing in constant use, as you may see on the public conveyances on our streets. In this established form २, the origin of the Arabic ٢, the horizontal form of the original having been made vertical, we have our own 2, which approximates to the current Indian form.

3. *Three*, both on the Indian Caves, and among the Chinese is, 三 which, when cursively united, through ३, becomes ३ as in the Maráthí script character. In the Arabic of the present day, this is ٣, the three limbs of the figure being used vertically, instead of horizontally in which form it would appear as ३. Our own 3 is nearer the Indian letter than the Arabic.

4. *Four* is represented in Chinese either by four horizontal bars, or, as is most commonly the case, by a square of this form, 四, including two diacritical marks, and named *sú*. One of the oldest Indian forms of four is also a square, as is evident from its duplication in ▭▭, the representative of eight, occurring in the Cave inscriptions. In the Indian languages the original, in cursive writing, has passed, through ▭ and ४, into ४, the form in which it now appears, from which our own 4 has been derived. ४, an ancient Indian form, occurring on the Bhilsa Topes, is five minus one, as will be seen from our next paragraph.

5. To show the origin of *five*, I must pass on, by anticipation, to the Chinese ten, which is merely a digital mark, 十, formed like the Etruscan or Roman X, to signify the completion of the numbers represented by the ten fingers, the great arithmetical indices of most nations. In the same way as V, the half of X, became the representative of five, so in the Indian languages, as seen on the oldest Cave and Coin Inscriptions, ⊣ and ⊢ (the representatives of the half of +

or ten) have become the representatives of *five*. In a cursive form, ⊣ through Ч, has become ५, the present representative of five in most of the Indian languages. Another Indian cursive form of ⊣ is ॾ, and of ⊢ is ঽ, which, with the addition of the two lines often put at the top in Indian writing, become ॾ and ऽ, the last of which agrees with our own 5, which was probably in use at one time among the Arabs, who now, as their typical form, use ۵, resolvable into three plus two, and most commonly abbreviated into ٥.

6. The original Arabic *six* was probably ٩, being five plus one; and, open at the top for abbreviation, it is now ٦. Our own 6 is merely an inversion of the original Arabic sign. The Indians now use ६, (the reversion of 3, in duplication), for six, as on our Bombay street carriages. Six, in Chinese, is 六, (*lo*), which does not seem to have been adopted by the Indians.

7. I am not able to throw any light on the formation of the figure for *seven*. On one of the Káralá Cave-inscriptions it occurs both in letters and figure. The figure, however, has been injured; and its precise original form is not now ascertainable. In the Indian typical script form, it is ७, resembling our nine. In Arabic it is ٧.

8. Several forms of *eight* occur on the Cave and Coin Inscriptions of Western India, the principal of which are ⊏⊐, ∞, and ⊓⊓ which throw light on our own 8, used by Boethius, showing, as I have already remarked, that it is the duplication of the original four, □. In Chinese, eight is 八, which, placed vertically, ⋜, is one of the Indian (Nágarí) forms of eight. In the Maráthí script character, it is ८, an abbreviation not only of the Nágarí, but probably of 8, made in this way ⋛, only half the letter being used. In Arabic it is ٨.

9. The oldest form of *nine* with which I am acquainted occurs on the Bhilsa Topes in Central India, so ably illustrated by Major Cunningham. It occurs as ⊕, in ⊕ ≡ (93). The ⊕ is ten minus one. Omitting the interior of the upper cipher, and making a cursive adaptation of the letter, that it may be formed without lifting the pen from the paper, it becomes ९, as in the Maráthí and other Indian writings. From the reversion of this, in the Arabic ٩, comes our own 9. The Chinese 九 seems not to have been used by the Indians, directly at least, though it appears to represent ten minus one. An ancient Indian form of nine, ꝏ, occurring on coins and copperplates, is a mere variant of ⊕.

10. *Ten*, as I have already mentioned, is 十 in the Chinese writing. The Indians, on availing themselves of this form, probably to avoid its being confounded with +, the oldest form of their letter K, (as seen on the Cave inscriptions), surrounded it with a cipher, making it ⊕. The inconvenience of this numeral led ultimately to the omission of its interior portion, giving the Indians, the Arabs, and ourselves, our present decimal cipher, o, of which the simple dot • in decimal fractions, first used by the Indians, is only a further abbreviation. Among the Arabs the • is used for o.

On the various systems of representing tens, hundreds, thousands, and so forth, by the Chinese, Indians, and other ancient eastern nations, I do not here enter; for the Indian inscriptions show that it was long before a conventional agreement in these matters was obtained. No adequate illustration can be made of them in a short compass.

The few observations which I have here made are intended merely to throw some light on the origin of our simple numerals. They militate against the theory of Mr. James Prinsep,—whose ingenuity in the decipherment of the ancient Indian alphabets has led to invaluable discoveries in Indian antiquities,—who was inclined to hold that the Indian figures have been derived from the inceptive letters of their Sanskrit names. [See Prinsep's Essays on Indian Antiquities, carefully and ably edited and illustrated by Mr. Edward Thomas, C. S.] Though the Indians have, in all probablity, borrowed some figures from the Chinese, they have greatly improved upon their original. It is from India, through the intermediation of the Arabs, probably that our own numeral system has been derived.

TABLE OF NUMERAL UNITS.

	1	2	3	4	5	6	7	8	9	10
Chinese Numerals	一	二	三	四	五	六	七	八	九	十
Indian Cave Numerals	−	=	≡	[illegible]	[illegible]	Not found.	Not found.	[illegible] ∞	⊕ [illegible]	⊕
Formation of Indian Script Numerals	I	[illegible]	[illegible]	[illegible]	[illegible]			8 [illegible]	⊕	⊕ ○
Indian Script Numerals (Modi)	[illegible]	2	3	[illegible]	[illegible]	[illegible]*	[illegible]	[illegible]	[illegible]	∘
Indian Numerals (Nágarí)	१	२	३	४	५	६	७	८	९	•
Arabian Numerals	١	٢ [illegible]	٣ [illegible]	٤ [illegible]	[illegible]	٦	٧	٨	٩	•
European Numerals :—										
Sacra Bosco (died 1256)	*1*	[illegible]	*3*	[illegible]	[illegible]	*6*	∧	*8*	*9*	*0*
Roger Bacon (died 1292)	*1*	[illegible]	*3*	[illegible]	[illegible]	*6*	∧	*8*	*9*	*0*
Common European Script Numerals	*1*	*2*	*3*	[illegible]	*5*	*6*	*7*	*8*	*9*	*0*
Common European Numerals	1	2	3	4	5	6	7	8	9	0

* Inversion of [illegible]